The Day
My Heart
Turned Blue

The Day
My Heart
Turned Blue

Healing After the Loss of My Mother

Karla J Noland

www.revealhealthrive.com

The Day My Heart Turned Blue
Healing After the Loss of My Mother
Copyright © 2021 by Karla J. Noland

Printed in the United States of America.

Scripture quotations marked (NIV) are taken from the Holy Bible, New International Version®, NIV®. Copyright © 1973, 1978, 1984, 2011 by Biblica, Inc.™ Used by permission of Zondervan. All rights reserved worldwide. www.zondervan.comThe "NIV" and "New International Version" are trademarks registered in the United States Patent and Trademark Office by Biblica, Inc.™

Scripture quotations marked MSG are taken from THE MESSAGE, copyright © 1993, 2002, 2018 by Eugene H. Peterson. Used by permission of NavPress, represented by Tyndale House Publishers. All rights reserved.

Although the author and publisher have made every effort to ensure that the information in this book was correct at press time, the author and publisher do not assume and hereby disclaim any liability to any party for any loss, damage, or disruption caused by errors or omissions, whether such errors or omissions result from negligence, accident, or any other cause.

Adherence to all applicable laws and regulations, including international, federal, state, and local governing professional licensing, business practices, advertising, and all other aspects of doing business in the US, Canada, or any other jurisdiction, is the sole responsibility of the reader and consumer.

Neither the author nor the publisher assumes any responsibility or liability whatsoever on behalf of the consumer or reader of this material. Any perceived slight of any individual or organization is purely unintentional. The resources in this book are provided for informational purposes only and should not be used to replace the specialized training and professional judgment of a health care or mental health care professional. Neither the author nor the publisher can be held responsible for the use of the information provided within this book. Please always consult a trained professional before making any decision regarding treatment of yourself or others.

Published by Reveal Heal Thrive LLC
PO Box 52341
Durham, NC 27717

ISBN: 978-1-7374981-0-0 (hardcover)
ISBN: 978-1-7374981-1-7 (paperback)
ISBN: 978-1-7374981-2-4 (ebook)

Library of Congress Control Number: 2021918675

Dedication

In loving memory of my mommy, Eutrice Elsie James. Thank you for your unfailing love, earnest prayers, and unshakeable faith. Until we meet again, rest well in heaven. I will take it from here!

Contents

PART 3: GIVE YOURSELF PERMISSION

Introduction

I have always kept a diary or journal throughout my childhood and in my adult life. I write out my prayers, all the emotions I'm feeling, and dreams that seem unattainable at the moment. My journal entries express my pain, trauma, and insecurities. After my mother, Eutrice E. James, died on November 27th 2019, I discovered she had a collection of thirteen journals. Inside her journals, she chronicled her life experiences, personal prayers, and intercessory prayers for others.

I found comfort in my sorrow by reading my mother's journals. I learned so much about her personal conflicts, the extent of her faith, love, and her benevolent heart. For the first time, I viewed my mother as more than just my proud Trinidadian mom, but also as a beautiful soul cloaked in complexity and so deserving of the same kindness, compassion, and love that she poured out to others. It was heartbreaking to read how critical she was of herself. Several of her journal entries contained a tone of guilt, remorse, and regret. She never thought she was good enough or intelligent enough to accomplish big things. And yet, despite my mother's inner struggles, she has touched many people's lives and should be honored with the same love she freely gave to others. Unbeknownst to her, she did accomplish big things. My mother's journal writings left a legacy of faith, love, family, and service to all who need encouragement and hope.

Gratitude is a common theme throughout my mother's journals. She constantly expresses her undying gratitude to her Lord and Savior, Jesus Christ. Her faith stood on the principles of Christianity, but I affectionately call her a Christ follower. I can't remember a time when my mother didn't give God the glory for all He did in her life.

I am a Christ follower because of my mother's faith as well. I accepted Christ into my life at ten years old, and I do not know who or where I would be without my faith in Jesus. At my best and my lowest, God is always with me. I know who I am in Christ Jesus and that He loves me more than I could ever imagine. There is nothing I could do to stop God from loving me.

> *And I am convinced that nothing can ever separate us from God's love. Neither death nor life, neither angels nor demons, neither our fears for today nor our worries about tomorrow—not even the powers of hell can separate us from God's love. No power in the sky above or in the earth below—indeed, nothing in all creation will ever be able to separate us from the love of God that is revealed in Christ Jesus our Lord.*
>
> (Romans 8:38-39, NIV)

I wrote *The Day My Heart Turned Blue* for people who are reeling from the death of a parent and need encouragement to move forward. The collective journal writings and prayers of my beloved mother, Eutrice E. James, speak volumes about the power of journaling. May her handwritten words of faith and service to others encourage you in your time of grief. As you read *The Day my Heart Turned Blue*, may it inspire you to write and share your own life experiences, revealing your stifled emotions so that you can heal and thrive in life.

The stories in this book reflect the journal entries of the recollection of events from my mother's point of view. Dialogue has been re-created from her memory based on the content written in her journal entries.

Part 1

Picking up the Pieces

"You don't get over it, you just get through it. You don't get by it, because you can't get around it. It doesn't 'get better,' it just gets different. Everyday grief puts on a new face."

—Wendy Feireisen

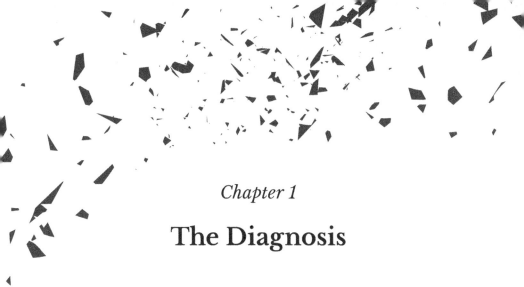

Chapter 1

The Diagnosis

At seventy-seven years old, my Trinidadian mother was the epitome of health. She was a retired Clinical Dietitian from The University of Texas MD Anderson Cancer Center in Houston, Texas. After retirement, she spent much of her time volunteering at Sagemont Church, spending time with her grandchildren, friends, and family, and caring for her beloved herb, fruit, and vegetable garden. She also loved to cook, travel, and go on mission trips around the world. My mother kept a healthy lifestyle and bragged about her ability to walk five to seven miles three times a week for exercise. Her favorite color was blue. I can no longer look at the color blue without thinking about my mother.

Although my mother complained about lower back pain for five years, it never stopped her from doing what she loved. Eventually, however, she went to the doctor and discovered that she had a spot on her spine, and her doctor decided to monitor it. Later, in 2016, she got into a car accident with an 18-wheeler. While she had no injuries (by the grace of God), an MRI showed that the spot on her lower back had grown to the size of a blueberry. She assured me there was no need to be alarmed, and I trusted her.

Then, in 2018 and early 2019, my mother complained of knee pain, and her doctor suggested she have knee replacement surgery and reduce the number of miles she walked. I assumed this was a standard operating procedure considering her age and active lifestyle. However, the knee replacement left the bottom of my mother's foot numb, and physical therapy did not help with the numbness. As a result, she had to use a cane for walking and had reduced movement in her knee and foot. It frustrated her to be unable to move around the way she used to.

In July 2019, I traveled with my youngest son from my home in Durham, North Carolina, to visit my mother for a few weeks and celebrate my birthday with her and my friends in Houston, Texas. I worked remotely from my mother's home during my visit while she went back and forth to the doctor to investigate the numbness in her foot. On one occasion, she wanted me to go with her to the doctor, but I had a work meeting scheduled simultaneously, and I was watching both my son and the child of a family friend. I didn't want to haul the children to her appointment, so I reassured my mother that she could just go alone and tell me all about it when she got back. When my mother returned from her appointment, she told me the doctor strongly suggested surgery and that she would consider it. In the meantime, she wanted to spend time with her youngest grandson, so I flew back home to Durham for much-needed "me time" and spending quality childfree time with my husband.

Looking back, I wish I had gone to that doctor's appointment to find out what was going on with the numbness in my mother's leg sooner. I often wonder: Could I have made a difference if I had known more about her medical condition earlier? I would never have thought that would be the last birthday I would spend with my mother.

I was willing to fly back to Houston to pick up my son after his summer visit with Grandma, but my mother insisted on bringing him back to Durham herself because she wanted to see him off for his first day of school (2nd grade) and spend the remainder of August with us. When I picked my mother up from the airport, I noticed her health had deteriorated. Any time she would visit me in North Carolina, she cooked my favorite Trinidadian meals such as callaloo, accra, stewed chicken, peas and rice, and bacalao, to name a few. But this visit was different. I knew she wasn't herself. She was in severe pain and unable to walk up and down steps with ease. She slept more, used narcotic painkillers, and asked for an ice pack around the clock to numb her back. By the end of the summer, she could not walk without the assistance of a cane or do everyday tasks on her own.

There was nothing left to consider. My mother needed to have back surgery.

In August 2019, my mother decided to have surgery and made arrangements to schedule the procedure for September. I dropped her off at the airport in a wheelchair and brought her to the gate for departure. I told her I would visit her afterward, but I didn't make plans right away because it did not resonate with me that this would be major surgery. I thought my mother was healthy and vibrant; she had already had two knee surgeries and would be fine. I figured the doctor would remove the blueberry-sized mass from her back, and she would be back on her feet once again. I viewed my mother as strong and invincible. If she could survive a crash with an 18-wheeler, she could certainly get through another surgery.

It was my mother's last visit to North Carolina and our last embrace before the surgery. It was also the last time my mother would have one-on-one time with her grandson in her home. When I reflect on this, I realize the importance of being present in the moment and spending quality time with our loved ones because you never know when it will be the last time you see them.

When my mother arrived back home in Houston, her pain worsened, and she was prescribed opioids to ease her pain. Before surgery, she'd had to undergo several biopsies and tests to determine if the mass on her lower back was cancerous. It was a full-circle moment for her because her surgery took place at The University of Texas MD Anderson Cancer Center, where she retired as a clinical dietician. My mother informed me all tests came back negative for cancer. The relief in her voice put my mind at ease that everything was going to be okay.

I never thought my mother's health would take a turn for the worse the way it did. I waited patiently for a phone call from my mom on how she made it through surgery. However, she didn't call me. Another family member reached out to me instead. I cannot remember who called me, but I do remember hearing the diagnosis of Primary Central Nervous System (CNS) melanoma. *Primary CNS melanomas are rare, and they constitute about 1% of all cases of melanomas and 0.07% of all brain tumors. These tumors are aggressive in nature and may metastasize to other organs. To date, less than 25 cases have been reported in the literature. The survival rate is 10 weeks once the cancer spreads to other organs.*[1] Primary CNS can go undetected in biopsies and prelab tests, which happened in my mother's case.

Strangely, my mother was in good spirits despite her diagnosis. She continued to give God the praise because she had finally found out what was causing the pain and numbness in her legs. However, my relatives, who were standing at her bedside, had a different tone. I felt the sadness from them over the phone. I wasn't sure if I should drop everything and take the next flight to Houston or not because my mother still had a positive attitude. She never talked about how she felt or if she thought death was imminent, nor did she give me any updates on her medical condition after the surgery. She only spoke about what she had for breakfast, lunch, and dinner, and lighthearted chit-chat.

I believe this was her way of protecting me from the truth of her situation. I still do not know which stage of cancer she was diagnosed with; I can only assume it was stage IV. Shock doesn't describe what I felt when I got the news. I heard the word *cancer*, but I could not process what I heard because my mother lived such a healthy lifestyle. She didn't eat processed foods, drink alcohol heavily, or smoke. How could she get cancer? I trusted God for a miracle, but my heart was heavy with the weight of what felt like a predestined outcome.

Chapter 2

Happy Birthday, Mommy

My mother would not give me any information regarding her medical condition, so my aunt took the lead by helping me stay in communication with the doctors. She also kept me updated on my mother's health; we video chatted from my mother's bedside so I could see her face, and my aunt encouraged me to keep the faith. I am eternally grateful for my aunt being such a gracious caregiver to my mother during this difficult time.

Instead of keeping me updated about her health, my mother chose to tell me stories about all the visitors who had come to her bedside and how well she was treated at MD Anderson Cancer Center. She seemed surprised to receive so many visitors. I don't believe my mom realized how loved and appreciated she was for her service to others.

She also made several phone calls to friends and family. She even reached out to my ex-husband (the father of my older two sons). At the time, I couldn't figure out why she would call him when she could reach out to her grandchildren directly. She also communicated with Dad, though she didn't tell me the details of their conversation. As I reflect on these memories, I believe my mom knew she was dying and wanted to give her last words to everyone she had as a contact in her phone.

Radiation was the next step after my mother's Primary CNS Diagnosis. My mother seemed disoriented afterward. She wasn't her usual upbeat self and did not talk as much over the phone. Once her treatment was complete, she was transferred to a nursing home and rehabilitation center for in-patient physical therapy, but she did not improve.

I flew out to Houston to visit her at the nursing home and rehabilitation center for her 78th birthday on October 26, 2019. It was the first time I saw my mother since she visited me in North Carolina in late August 2019. Once I arrived at the airport, I got a ride to my mother's home, picked up her car, and drove straight to the rehabilitation center. I called my best friend, Tamara, on the way there because the closer I got to the medical center, the more anxious I felt. She wanted to meet me at the rehabilitation center to be my support system. I am so grateful for our friendship of over 25 years.

As I made a left turn onto the street of the rehabilitation center, I remembered a previous phone call with my cousin. She had seen my mom before I did and broke into tears in the middle of our conversation. She told me that the woman she'd seen was not her aunt, and her words haunted me as I pulled into the parking lot. I got out of the car and broke out in a nervous sweat as I entered the lobby, looking for someone to point me in the right direction of my mother. The front desk attendant directed me to the dining hall.

I saw my mother sitting in a wheelchair as I entered the dining hall. Her body was frail, and her feet looked severely swollen from sitting in the same posture for a long time. And yet, when our eyes met, she had the biggest smile on her face.

"Mommy!" I cried out. I ran to her, bent down, and placed my head on her chest like I was five years old again. Then I began to cry because I realized my mother was dying. I was heartbroken because my worst fear had become a terrible, inevitable reality.

Eventually, I dried my tears because I did not want my mother to feel bad on her birthday. Other residents surrounded us at the dining hall table, and I didn't want to ruin the mood for everyone. It was lunchtime, and they were having ice cream afterward to celebrate my mother on her special day. Ice cream was her favorite dessert.

I pulled up a chair, sat next to my mom, and looked at her more closely. Her hands looked contracted and bent, and she could no longer stand or walk. Just as my mother had fed me as a small child, I had to feed her lunch that day because she had lost the use of her hands. Also, we could not have a conversation the way we had done in the past because her speech was limited. However, her spirit was still strong. In true motherly fashion, she reminded me not to spill ice cream on her birthday blouse as I fed her.

Tamara showed up at this time, and we laughed and giggled with the residents as if everything was great. I appreciate her for lightening the mood with her comedic timing. Also, a hilarious resident kept us in stitches with her jokes about other residents and the staff. She "spilled all the tea" about how the food was horrible and even had her brother bring BBQ for everyone. Laughter is truly medicine for the soul. For a brief moment, I forgot about my mother's failing health and enjoyed our conversation at the table.

After lunch, we played bingo with the residents. I noticed that my mother's hands trembled as she attempted to pick up a bingo chip and find the number to place the chip on the board. It was painful to sit and observe my mother in this state. These same hands used to part and braid my hair with precision and without a strand out of place. These same hands planted seeds in her backyard, which grew into herbs, vegetables, and a papaya tree. These hands bathed and swaddled her children, grandchildren, and great-nieces and nephews. And now, these hands were unable to put chips on a bingo card. Sadness overwhelmed me, but I kept a smiling face for my mother. I placed the chips on the card for her, and to her surprise, she won! Her winning prize was a bag of potato chips.

At this point, it was time for Tamara to leave, so I left my mother briefly and walked her outside. I immediately turned to her and cried on her shoulder. Tamara responded to my tears with a hug and the empathetic statement, "I know, Girl, I know." She felt the pain of my brokenness because I couldn't hold my sadness in any longer. I wiped my tears to thank her for being there for me and reassured her we would connect again before I went back to North Carolina. I got myself together once again to be strong for my mom and went back inside.

The facility had an outside garden and sitting area, so I wheeled my mother outside to get some fresh air. Unfortunately, I have little experience pushing wheelchairs, and I accidentally hit my mother's foot on the door. She had no feeling left in her legs, but I lifted her foot out of concern and asked if she was okay.

My mother comedically whispered, "You hit my foot on the door and asked me if I was okay?" We both laughed.

While we were outside, we gazed at the flowers, and the warm Texas sun shone on my mother's face. She admired the beauty of the sunflowers and magnolia trees. I asked her how she was feeling, and she replied, "Good." I did not push her further, but I knew she wasn't good. I wanted her to tell me the truth. I wanted to know how she felt, knowing that her time was drawing near. I wanted to know if she was scared. Was she mad at God? Did she blame herself for her condition? I wanted her to tell me how I could help her. But I knew I would not get these answers.

The only thing I knew to do at that moment was pray. I held my mother's hand and prayed that God's will would be done and that He would give us "the peace that transcends all understanding," as stated in His Word. I prayed for the strength only God could provide at that moment to accept the things we could not change. As I ended my prayer, my mother whispered, "Thank you," and I replied, "I love you," and I reached in and kissed her on her cheek.

At dinner time, I pushed her back to her room because she was not hungry. The room was drab with pale green and yellow color pallets from the seventies. I brought pictures of my children and special moments we shared to fill her room with life. I recorded her on video as she stared at each photo in the book I'd created. I had to help her turn each page, and she had trouble formulating words and recognizing shapes. I showed her a picture of me on a hike, and she mistook a tree for a monkey. We both got a good laugh out of that. But in my heart, I knew that cancer had already spread to her brain.

We waited a while for someone to help her get back into her bed, and then I stood in the hallway looking for someone to help us. There wasn't anyone in sight. I left my mom briefly to go to the nursing station to ask for help. There was one nurse at the nursing station. She explained there were only two nursing assistants on the late shift, one for each facility wing.

My God, I thought. *An estimated 60 patients temporarily lived there, and only two nurses' aides were available to prepare each patient for bed?!* I couldn't believe it. My mother had warned me about putting her in a nursing home when she got old. She always told me how horrible the conditions were in some places. Now, all these years later, I realized what she meant, and it infuriated me.

Eventually, one of the nursing assistants, a young African-American woman, came into my mother's room. She informed me it was a two-person job to place a patient on the lift to remove them from their wheelchair and place them in the bed. There was a chance the patient could fall if she didn't have another set of hands to assist with the transition, and she asked if I could help. I agreed and supported my mother as she was lifted out of her wheelchair. Once my mother was in the air, I observed how the nursing assistant used the lift machine to place my mother gently into her bed. Once she was settled, the nursing assistant changed her diaper, took off her birthday clothes, and dressed her in pajamas.

As I watched, I reflected on my mother's evening routine when she had been healthy. She would brush her teeth, wash her face, and use a nighttime moisturizer. She often put her hair in rollers before she went to bed as well. Those days now felt like a distant memory.

At that point, the nurse, a slightly older African-American woman, interrupted my thoughts as she came into the room yelling, "It's time for your medicine, Ms. James."

The nursing assistant propped up my mother so that she could take her pills while the nurse attempted to put them into my mother's mouth. My mother furiously spat out the pain medication in protest. It was the first time that day that I had seen her move any part of her body with such force. In the end, the nurse had to force my mom to take her medicine, which brought me to tears. I couldn't understand why she refused her treatment, and my mother could not (or would not) explain why she didn't want it. Maybe she didn't like the taste or thought it would make her condition worse; I don't know. The funny resident told me that when my mother didn't take her pain medicine, she was talkative and lively, but she seemed more lethargic when she took it. I don't know for sure if my mother felt that way or not.

When the nurse and the nurse's aide left my mother's room, I kissed my mother good night and left. As I drove away, my heart felt like it had broken into tiny pieces. I kept thinking about my day with my mother and how she was literally dying before my eyes. In a way, grief took hold of me way before my mother took her last breath. I couldn't grapple with the fact that I couldn't communicate with her the way I wanted. I wanted to know what she was feeling. Did her brain hurt? What were her prayers to God at that moment? Did she know all along that the pain in her back would eventually lead to her death? Had she kept that secret to herself for all these years?

I would never get the answers to those questions. All I could do at that moment was cry. Each tear shed was a gut check that I did not have long with my mother. I called my husband's aunt and asked her to pray for me. She, too, is a woman of unshakeable faith in my life and has the prophetic gift through prayer. She cried out to God in prayer on my behalf and re-assured me my mother's condition was out of my hands and God's will. After her prayer, I leaned into the uncertainty that God was in control of the situation. I had to come to terms with the fact that my mother's time on earth was coming to an end.

I had wanted my mother to stay in her home after her surgery. I hated leaving her in a nursing home and rehabilitation center because I knew she never wanted to spend the rest of her days there. However, my mom required 24-hour care with machinery to get her in and out of bed. That type of care was too costly and not covered under Medicare or private health insurance. According to the National Academy of Elder Law Attorneys (NAELA), most people who need such care for extended periods will even-tually deplete their assets and become unable to pay the costs of their care[1]. Many people do not realize the number of gaps in insurance coverage between their elderly parents' private insurance and Medicare regarding their failing health.

I made a few calls to my mother's private insurance company and Medicare. Both organizations made it clear that they did not pay for room and board at nursing homes, only my mother's medical needs. After do-ing some research, I found that in 2019, the national median for monthly nursing home costs was $7,513 for a shared room and $8,517 for a private room, according to a 2019 Genworth Cost of Care Survey. That is eas-ily $95,000–$100,000 dollars a year. If your elderly parent qualifies for Medicaid, their local state government will pay for their long-term care expenses. However, Medicaid eligibility is based on a person's monthly in-come, which may include a pension, Social Security, and other payments, in addition to "countable" assets[2].

In my opinion, you have to be dead broke, for lack of a better word, to get Medicaid benefits. When you apply for them, there is a five-year "look-back" at all asset transfers, and if Medicaid finds that money has been transferred within the last five years, a penalty period is imposed, delaying the onset of coverage [2]. The healthcare system in the U.S. makes me so angry. You can go broke trying to pay for long-term elderly care and get penalized at the same time for being financially responsible and saving money throughout your life.

Since my mother owned her own home and had a pension, 401K, etc., she did not qualify for Medicaid. My only option was to cover her room and board at my own expense because my mother did not have the savings to pay for them. To get the ball rolling, my aunt and uncle set my mom up at the nursing home for her first week, which was the last week of the month. However, I had to pay for her room and board fees a month in advance from that point on.

When I returned to North Carolina, I took out a $20,000 loan against my 401K as an act of faith to pay for my mother's room and board for the next four months. Once I received the check, I went to the bank to deposit it into my bank account. When the bank teller asked about my plans for the money, I broke down and cried at her station. The bank teller (named Star) reassured me that everything would work out because I was doing it for my mother. I took her name as a sign that God would be my guiding light through that entire process. I trusted God to show me how I would pay my monthly bills and repay a $20,000 loan at the same time.

Consequently, I never had to pay a month in advance for my mother's room and board. God had other plans for the money. A week later, my mother's health took a turn for the worse. Her rehabilitation efforts failed, and her doctor submitted paperwork to move her to a hospice care facility. Ironically, Medicaid pays 100% for elderly Hospice care when an elderly patient is dying, regardless of their income.

Hospice care is a special kind of care that focuses on the quality of life for people and their caregivers who are experiencing an advanced, life-limiting illness. Hospice care provides compassionate care for people in the last phases of incurable disease so that they may live as fully and comfortably as possible.

The hospice philosophy accepts death as the final stage of life: It affirms life but does not try to hasten or postpone death. Hospice care treats the person and symptoms of the disease, rather than treating the disease itself. A team of professionals work together to manage symptoms so that a person's last days may be spent with dignity and quality, surrounded by their loved ones. Hospice care is also family-centered—it includes the patient and the family in making decisions [3].

> *"You matter because of who you are. You matter to the last moment of your life, and we will do all we can, not only to help you die peacefully, but also to live until you die."*
>
> —Dame Cicely Saunders,
founder of the first modern hospice

Chapter 3

Her Last Breath

"Life is not measured by the number of breaths we take, but the moments that take our breath away."

—Unknown

A week before Thanksgiving, my aunt called me and said my mother didn't have much time left, and the nurse on call at the hospice facility said I should come right away. I booked a flight to Houston the next day for my husband, our youngest son, and myself. We stayed at my mother's house as we traveled back and forth to the hospice facility to sit at her bedside. By this time, cancer had ravished my mother's body. She no longer had any body fat and was down to skin and bones. The doctor placed her in an induced coma to help her breathe more comfortably and keep her relaxed.

I put on a gospel playlist and placed my phone by her ear. I'd read somewhere that patients who are in a coma can still hear music. I sat on one side of my mother, my aunt sat on the other, and my husband sat at the foot of the bed. Our seven-year-old son focused on his tablet and stayed behind the curtain. I didn't want him to spend too much time looking at his grandmother in her weakened condition. I was concerned the sight of her diminished body would scare him.

I'd never paid as much attention to the act of breathing as I did when I was at my mother's bedside that day. She was hooked up to an oxygen mask to help her with her breathing, and I held her hand and observed every breath she took. The tubing that connected the oxygen mask went under her chin, which allowed her mouth to open and close. With each breath she took, I recalled a special memory that we shared, and as she released that breath, she reminded me that she was still with me in spirit.

My mom took a breath in, and I recalled the day I went into labor with my first child, her first grandson. She watched me push him into the world and take his first breath. She choked up with emotion and had to leave the room to cry. I will always have that special moment with my mother, and I clenched her hand as I watched her release her breath.

As she took another breath in, I remembered when she visited my family during the Christmas holidays. My husband and I were folding laundry. We found a pair of underwear that said, "Santa's Little Helper," and we couldn't figure out whose underwear it was. It turns out that it was my mom's! The three of us laughed so hard that day. As my mom released her breath, she reminded me that her spirit was still with me.

She took another breath in, and I remembered a conversation we had in August 2019. She looked at me and said she was proud of me for all that I had overcome and that I still could keep going. Then, as she lay on the bed in front of me, she released her breath.

On November 27th, 2019, I watched my mother take her last breath. She died with dignity and a smile on her face.

At this moment, the circle of life was clear to me. Forty-three years ago, my mom went into labor with me and brought me into this world. She saw my first breath, and I was present to watch her take her last.

Oddly enough, relief came over my body because my mother was no longer in pain or suffering. She was with God, and her pain was now over. I held my mother's hand one last time, but this time, her body was lifeless, even though it still felt warm. I took a picture of us holding hands one last time to remind me how I reached for her hand as a little girl to help me feel safe, secure, and loved.

As painful as that moment was for me, my faith reminded me that *to be absent from the body is to be with the Lord* (2 Corinthians 5:8). My mother lived every day for God. She was His humble servant while here on earth, and now she is reunited with her creator. She no longer has a body made of skin and bones, but she now has a heavenly body. A friend from church shared with me that she had a vision of my mother with angel wings. I am blessed to be surrounded by so many friends and family who are rooted in the Christian faith. I now picture my supernatural mother clothed in heavenly white robes with beautiful blue, silver, and white-trimmed wings, continuing to do God's work but now in heaven.

> *For we know that when this earthly tent we live in is taken down (that is, when we die and leave this earthly body), we will have a house in heaven, an eternal body made for us by God himself and not by human hands. We grow weary in our present bodies, and we long to put on our heavenly bodies like new clothing. For we will put on heavenly bodies; we will not be spirits without bodies. While we live in these earthly bodies, we groan and sigh, but it's not that we want to die and get rid of these bodies that clothe us. Rather, we want to put on our new bodies so that these dying bodies will be swallowed up by life. God himself has prepared us for this, and as a guarantee, he has given us his Holy Spirit. So, we are always confident, even though we know that as long as we live in these bodies, we are not at home with the Lord. For we live by believing and not by seeing. Yes, we are fully confident, and we would rather be away from these earthly bodies, for then we will be at home with the Lord. So, whether we are here in this body or away from this body, our goal is to please him.*
>
> (2 Corinthians 5:1-9, NIV)

Chapter 4

The Dance Between Grief and Duty: Planning the Funeral

S hortly after my mother took her last breath, my aunt stayed behind to wait for the funeral home to pick up my mother's body from the hospice facility. She suggested the rest of us get something to eat and meet back at my mother's house. I'm glad she did that because I don't know how I would have reacted to seeing the funeral home put my mother in a body bag, place her on a gurney, and take her away. My husband, son, and I met my best friend at a local Pho restaurant. We made small talk over our meal, never stating the obvious about what had just happened. I was relieved my mother was no longer in pain, but I was still shocked that I had seen her pass away.

Next, the funeral home needed us to pick out my mother's clothes for her burial, so when we got back to her house, we went through her closet and looked for what we thought would be the perfect dress. My mother's favorite color was blue, but we couldn't find the perfect blue dress for her. Instead, I found a white dress suit trimmed in gold and a gold pair of shoes to match. My aunt joked that my mother wouldn't need shoes because her feet would be hidden in the coffin. Still, I knew that my mother would want to be well-dressed from head to toe with pantyhose, shoes, and her favorite jewelry.

As we gathered the items, I remembered my mother pointing me to the location of her will and other essential documents for when she passed away. I didn't take the conversation too seriously because my mother would live to be 100+ years old in my mind. She was the healthiest 78-year-old woman I have ever known. If I had the chance to have the conversation again, I would have asked her more questions regarding her funeral service. What outfit did she want to wear as we laid her to rest? How did she want her hair styled? What picture did she want us to use for the program? What was her favorite bible verse? Which minister did she want to preside over the service? There wasn't much space for me to grieve at that moment because, as a family, we had to answer those questions ourselves and plan the funeral.

Once my aunt gathered all the necessary items for my mom's burial, it was time for my husband and me to talk to our youngest son about what happened. My mother's passing was a smooth transition; she died quietly and peacefully. As a result, my seven-year-old son was so engrossed in playing Roblox that he didn't even know his Grandma Eutrice had passed away. My heart was heavy with anxiety about having to tell my baby boy this sad news. As a parent, I did not want to break his heart.

My husband and I explained that Grandma Eutrice was sick and had just become an angel. My son's eyes got big when he realized what we meant by that. I do not remember him shedding one tear. However, I do remember him proclaiming, "That means she's in heaven with God!" I answered with an "Amen" and informed him he now had a grandma who was a guardian angel and watched over him from heaven. My baby boy's innocence and high IQ made our conversation a bit easier than I expected, but I knew it would be harder to tell my two older sons the same news.

The next day, I had an appointment with the funeral home to make arrangements for the service. My aunt, uncle, husband, and baby boy accompanied me. The receptionist directed us to a private room with a large oval table, a big-screen TV, flowers, several bottles of bottled water, and a card offering condolences for our loss. Eventually, two women entered the room and introduced themselves as the people who would preside over my mother's funeral arrangements. One was an African-American woman named Dawn, who had a comforting, empathetic tone. She told me she was responsible for everything "below ground" concerning the preparation of the body and the burial. The other was younger and Latina; her name was Marcela. She was in charge of the actual funeral service and all of the "above-ground" preparations.

As we conversed about the next steps, both women offered their condolences and told us they were sorry for our loss. My aunt replied, "Eutrice is not lost and are you really sorry because you are gaining financially from our so-called 'loss.'" I chuckled at my aunt's candidness; she had never been one to hold her tongue, and she wasn't about to stop now.

Dawn informed me that my mother had prepaid for her burial plot. However, I was responsible for paying for everything above ground, including the preparation and embalming of her body, the casket, funeral service, etc. My mother left out all of those details. She only told me to pick out her coffin, which didn't seem like a big deal until the time actually came to pick her coffin. Marcela gave me a pamphlet that displayed the available funeral packages. I felt like I was ordering a #1 combo with upgrade options from a fast-food restaurant. There was a wide variety of choices, including coffin finishes, flower arrangements, various food trays, and drinks available for the guests.

Most people probably don't understand the costs associated with funerals. According to the National Funeral Directors Association (NFDA), in 2019, the total median funeral costs exceeded $10,000[1]. I picked option #2, which wasn't the cheapest or the most expensive package to honor my mother with a beautiful service. Many people die without an insurance policy, which leaves the surviving family members to pay for the funeral. My mother did not have an insurance policy. The monetary death benefit I would receive as a part of her retirement benefits wasn't accepted by the funeral home due to how long it took to process the check. They rejected other insurance policies for the same reason. Thankfully, the $20,000 I had taken out of my 401K to cover my mother's costs at the nursing home now went toward covering her funeral costs. In other words, my previous act of faith had made it possible for me to pay for my mother's funeral without any distractions.

Dawn examined my mom's paperwork before the meeting. During our conversation, she pulled out a copy of my parent's divorce decree and pointed out a mistake. While my parents were married, they purchased the land for their burial plots. The court viewed this as property owned during the marriage. When my parents divorced, my dad gave his burial plot to my mother. However, the divorce decree stated that my dad owned both burial plots. To correct this error, he had to sign over the burial plot to me so I could bury my mother legally.

I set an appointment the next day for my dad to come to the funeral home to sign the necessary paperwork work for me. While we waited for the paperwork to be drafted, I turned to my dad and said, "Daddy, are your affairs in order when you die? Planning Mommy's funeral has been a lot for me to deal with mentally."

My father replied, "I prefer to be cremated, but don't worry. All arrangements have been made, including a primary and secondary contact who would be in charge of my estate." I breathed a sigh of relief. Then, as a family, we chose a date for the funeral with enough time for friends and family to travel and celebrate my mother's life.

My next step was to inform my two older boys about their beloved grandma's passing. Before speaking directly to my sons, I reached out to their paternal grandma and their father for support. I did not want my sons alone when I gave them the news. During this time, my oldest son was nineteen years old and in his freshman year of college as a student-athlete. I contacted his basketball coaches to inform them of his grandma's passing and explained that I would need them to surround him with love when I broke the news to him.

One of my mother's best friends invited us over for dinner with other close friends of the family. My husband and I decided it would be best to tell the boys with a support system nearby. I also called my ex-husband to inform him before I gave our sixteen-year-old son the news about his grandmother. I didn't want him alone as I gave him the news, so his dad was present during the video chat. I can't remember the exact words I told him; I only remember a tear from his right eye rolling down his cheek. My heart sank, but I knew I couldn't withhold the truth from him. I asked him if he wanted to attend her funeral. I wasn't sure how he would handle seeing his beloved grandmother, who held him in her arms, cooked his favorite meals, and who would show up at his school for Grandparent's Day, now lying in a coffin. He said he wanted to come to Houston to pay his respects, so his Dad agreed to accompany him on the flight to Houston.

Next, I called my oldest son. My mom had been there for his birth. I knew calling him would be the hardest for me; he didn't even want to hear the news initially about his grandmother having cancer. I reached out to his assistant basketball coach to coordinate the best time to talk and decided that our video chat would be in his office, so my son wouldn't have to internalize the news by himself. When I saw my son's face, I could tell he didn't know what I would say, but he seemed to recognize that since I'd pulled him into the office with his coach, it wasn't good.

Again, I don't remember the exact words I told him. I believe this is my brain's way of protecting itself from painful memories. However, I recall that after I told him about his grandmother, he buried his face in his arms as he leaned on the coach's desk. Tears flowed from my eyes because I had to deliver such devastating news to my child. I asked, "Would you like to come to the funeral?" He agreed, and his dad booked the flights for both of our boys.

I'm grateful to my son's assistant coach and his entire basketball team for surrounding him with love since I couldn't physically be there with him. I'm also grateful to my son's father for being there for our boys during this difficult time. We were together for 11 years and did not end our relationship on good terms. Still, at that moment, our co-parenting skills aligned as we put our children's emotional wellbeing above any negative feelings we may have had toward each other.

The Funeral

On the day of the funeral, I kept overthinking how I would react when I saw my mother's body lying in a coffin. The dramatic side of me wondered if I would cry uncontrollably or cling to the casket as my heart broke into tiny pieces. However, I didn't have much time to be dramatic because soon, my children arrived, along with their paternal grandmother, who came for support. Immediately I switched into mommy mode to protect their emotional wellbeing given the situation.

The boys' dad dropped them off at their grandmother's house. It was the first time their grandmother wasn't there to greet them at the door. As they walked into the house, the table in the foyer proudly displayed their baby pictures just as my mother had left it. After I greeted them and thanked their dad for accompanying them, they met several members of their Trinidadian side of the family for the first time. There were plenty of hugs to go around, which helped lighten the mood.

Since my boys arrived in town the same day as the funeral, there wasn't time to shop for traditional black suits. Instead, my sons wore their basketball gear from their respected schools. I reassured them their clothing attire was not a big deal. What was most important was that they had arrived in time to pay their respects to their grandma. I also didn't think their grandmother would have minded their funeral fashion because she enjoyed seeing her grandsons play basketball and traveled across the country to be with them. As a family, we decided to wear the color blue to honor my mother. Before getting sick, she told me she didn't want anyone looking sad at her funeral or wearing black because it was a celebratory time; she had reunited with her Heavenly Father.

My aunt, uncle, and cousins met us at my mom's house, and we traveled together in a caravan to the funeral. Immediate family was allowed to view the body first and had the chance to inform the funeral director of any last-minute changes before the funeral service began. As I inspected every inch of my mother's body lying in the casket, I thought to myself, *This is not my mother.* My mother's spirit no longer resided in the body I once knew. The body I stared at didn't even look like her. She was darker than usual, and it felt hard and cold. Her hair and makeup did not resemble anything I was used to seeing. I didn't think about purchasing a wig for my mother. Little details like buying wigs and makeup for African-American skin tones got lost in my anguish.

The night before, my friend's mother warned me that most funeral homes do not know how to apply makeup to Black skin. I laughed when she initially told me this, and laughed again when I saw the makeup on my mother's face. She was right; my mother's makeup was definitely the wrong shade, especially her lipstick. My aunt was visibly upset by this, but I didn't care because my mother was no longer in that body.

My cousin asked the funeral director if she had a curling iron to fix my mother's hair in order to remedy the situation. Before my mother was a clinical dietician, she was a cosmetologist. The thought of her getting her hair retouched in a coffin was comical to me. Watching my cousin curl my mother's natural hair with a 9mm barrel curling iron was the kind of funny moment that kept my spirits up. The curling iron was way too small to create bouncy curls on her curly, 4C hair type. I walked away in laughter while my cousin kept trying to add the curls with a curling iron that wasn't right for the job.

I decided to turn my attention to greeting guests. I wasn't in the mood to sit and be somber. Instead, I found myself operating as a hostess, welcoming friends, families, and all those who came to pay their respects at my mother's funeral. I wanted to shift the atmosphere from sorrow to joy. It was a time to honor the life of my mother, who was no longer lying in a hospice bed in a drug-induced coma. She was with her Heavenly Father in heaven, living her best eternal life.

My cousin set up a live Facebook feed from the funeral service so my family in Trinidad and Tobago could watch from afar. Once everything was in place, the service began. One of the pastors from my mother's church led the service, and there was a lineup of speakers to eulogize my mother's life. I spoke along with my mom's best friends and aunt.

As I approached the podium, I stared at the faces of the attendees. I could see how my mother's spirit had touched so many people regardless of race, ethnicity, gender, or age. I shared a story of how my mother never met a stranger. When I was younger, she gave everyone she encountered unsolicited advice. I would be so embarrassed as she spoke to everyone she met. However, there was never push back or disrespect. The people my mother met turned into newfound acquaintances who always nodded and said, "Yes, Ma'am," in agreement and smiled back at her.

Here on earth, my mother was an example of what it meant to be the "hands and feet" of God. What my mother had was yours. If you were hungry, she fed you. If you were discouraged, she encouraged you. If you needed a mom, aunt, or grandma, she embodied that as well! I reminded all those in attendance—along with our family watching from Trinidad and Tobago—that my mom was now an angelic spirit. Even after death, she would continue to inspire us to grow closer to God, help those in need, and love one another.

After the funeral service, we drove to my mom's burial site on the same property as the chapel. My mother's burial plot sat high on a hill, and we had to walk up the steps to get there. At the top of the steps was a pergola, a bench, flower bushes, and statues of cherubs to greet visitors, and on the right-hand side of the pergola, my mother was laid to rest. I couldn't have asked for a more beautiful spot.

My husband, my older two boys, my uncle, cousins, and close family members were my mother's pallbearers. A few of my high school and college classmates came to the gravesite to greet me and share their respects for my mother. I am so blessed to have such loving friends. Even on the saddest of days, they still managed to make me smile and laugh. I can't remember what happened next or what words were said as the casket lowered. Each family member, including my youngest son, took a white rose from the casket and dropped it onto my mother's coffin as it rested below ground. My heart wouldn't let me stay any longer after that, so I headed back to the funeral home for the wake.

Those of us who returned for the wake caught up with each other and took pictures. I hadn't seen many of the funeral attendees since I was a young girl in Houston, Texas, but I could feel the love for my mother in the room. As we wrapped things up, I thanked the funeral directors for everything they had done. Then, my entire family got into their vehicles to head out to a restaurant as a caravan once again. When I got into the car with my husband and children, I noticed that my youngest son was missing, but no one else did. How could they forget my baby boy? I ran back into the funeral home, and I found my son walking from the chapel. I asked him what he had been doing, and he said he was talking to Grandma. I was perplexed; he just saw us bury his grandmother. He'd dropped a white rose onto her coffin. At first, I thought maybe he meant my older two boys' paternal grandmother, but she was already in another car. I decided it was best not to ask any more questions. I had survived my mother's funeral without an emotional breakdown; I wasn't ready to hear that my youngest son could talk to dead people.

KEEP, SELL, DONATE, OR TRASH

In 2003, my mother got a new start through homeownership. She had longed for her own home and couldn't wait to start her herb and vegetable garden. She also loved to cook and entertain anyone who entered her home. Exquisite tea and dinner sets filled her China cabinet, some of which she'd bought during her travels abroad. Fifteen years later, I found myself packing up my mother's 1900-plus square foot home. Since her death was unexpected, my relatives and I had to pack up everything just how she left it.

Sorting, boxing, and bagging my mother's belongings to either keep, sell, donate, or throw away took up much of my time. As a family, we worked through the packing process by dividing and conquering different rooms of the house. I also relied heavily on my family and friends in Houston, Texas, to help me with the packing process because I lived in North Carolina.

I gained a better understanding of my mother's taste and preferences by going through her belongings. We combed through boxes of every Oprah Magazine she saved and newspaper clippings of her favorite presidents and historical events. I also found many special-edition magazines paying tribute to the British Royal Family, which she admired. All these items that she saved as memorabilia ended up on the curb for trash pickup.

As I filled each trash bag, I couldn't help but reflect on how hard we work for material items to wear or to beautify our homes, and upon death, you can take none of those items with you. The act of bagging and tagging my mother's things made me think about how I was living my life, and I experienced a paradigm shift in how I would live my life from that point forward. The impact we leave behind is more important than the belongings we hold dear. Those belongings we leave behind always remain for someone else to decide what gets sold, donated, or thrown away.

My mother's bedroom was the most challenging room to pack because it represented the most intimate parts of her life. Tucked away in her closet were plastic bins with beautiful dresses she had sewn herself. She also had a collection of shoes she was proud of, all attributed to her upbringing. My mother often reminded me that she only had three pairs of shoes as a little girl growing up in Trinidad and Tobago: one pair of shoes for school, another for church, and a third pair for outside. I could still smell my mother's scent on her bedding and clothing. Her vanity and nightstands were just as she left them, with her favorite photographs, jewelry, and perfumes on display.

My mom's nightstand drawers held several journals she wrote in for the past 20 years. I didn't care if it took me another 20 years to read them all. I wanted to learn about everything that happened in my mother's life that she never told me. I always felt that she withheld so much from me to protect me, and reading her journals was a way for me to feel connected to her until we met again.

None of my mother's belongings held significance to her anymore because she was no longer here. What she treasured on earth was nothing more than stuff to anyone else. It would have been unreasonable for me to keep more than I could carry back to North Carolina. I held on to her handmade dresses and souvenirs from her mission trips to Kenya and Spain. We wore the same size in clothing and shoes, but we had unique tastes. However, I kept a few of her dresses and shoes for myself. To this day, whenever I miss my mom, I can put on a pair of her shoes and feel as though I'm literally and metaphorically standing in her shoes. I also kept her journals and Bibles, which I treasure. I believe these items represent the very essence of who she was on earth.

Executrix Duties

I didn't have much time to give myself space to grieve after the funeral because I was named the executrix of my mother's estate. An executrix is a female executor of a will. I knew nothing about this process, and it scared me. My mother never walked me through the responsibilities of her estate after the will. All I knew was to go to the Register of Deeds office with the will in hand to get clarity about the next steps.

My husband and youngest son accompanied me to the Register of Deeds office. I waited anxiously to be called by the next available clerk and explain my case. I didn't know what to expect. The clerk waved me over, and I shared that my mother had passed away and left a will naming me as the executrix. The clerk explained that I had to follow the probate process in Texas, which required me to hire a probate attorney. *Probate is the process in which a court legally recognizes a person's death and oversees the payment of a deceased person's debts and the distribution of his or her assets. The court's role is* to facilitate this process and protect, when necessary, the interests of all creditors and beneficiaries of the estate. The role of the Texas probate court and all persons hired by the court to facilitate this process is known as probate administration[2].

I could not represent myself in a Texas probate court, and I was not a Texas resident. Instantly, I knew I was in for a complicated process. I left the Register of Deeds office in tears. I felt lost, broken, and ill-equipped to handle my duties, but I didn't want to let my mother down. I cried in my husband's arms and prayed for direction about the next steps because I had no clue what to do.

After praying, I remembered a recent post from a friend on my social media page. She said she was praying for me and had gone through the same process with both sets of grandparents. I reached out to ask if she had any recommendations for a probate attorney and for advice about the process of selling my mother's home and belongings. God showed up and showed out for me again because my friend talked me through the entire process and gave me the number of the probate attorneys who had handled her grandparents' estate.

I called the probate attorney's office, explained the details of my mother's passing, and asked about my next steps. I also wanted to know the costs associated with their services. I was stunned by the fee, which can vary depending on the complexity of the estate. For me, the total fell within the range of $2,000–$10,000, depending on my case and a fee for a consultation. I hung up the phone. I didn't have an additional $10,000 to pay for my mother's affairs.

I prayed again, asking God for guidance and direction because I was running out of both options and money. I decided to post on social media again, asking for more friends to share recommendations of probate attorneys they had worked with, and I left it in God's hands.

When we returned to my mother's home, I was still upset about how to handle things. My aunt, uncle, and mother-in-law from my prior marriage were still at the house. I explained to them everything I had been told at the Register of Deeds office. I also got several recommendations from my social media page. My former mother-in-law said she would make some phone calls to the recommended attorneys for me and screen them. She also wrote on a notepad all the questions I had regarding the will and selling my mother's home and belongings. I sincerely appreciated her clear-headedness and logic in the situation because I was emotionally sinking from sadness and responsibility. We narrowed it down to three probate attorneys, but only one could meet with us the following day. We scheduled an appointment for the attorney to meet us at my mother's house. I felt relieved that I was headed in a positive direction concerning my executrix duties.

The next day, the probate attorney, an African-American woman, arrived right on time, and we met in my mother's office. She was so kind and empathic to my situation and offered her condolences right away. She had an excellent teaching tone as she walked my uncle, husband, and me through the Texas probate process. She explained what we could expect, how long it would take, and she broke down what the will meant in handling my mother's estate. She put my mind at ease, and I wanted to hire her right away, especially when she gave me the flat fee for her services, which was reasonable. I was ready to write a check. My uncle, husband, and I excused ourselves and discussed whether we should go forward with hiring her, and the three of us came to an agreement.

I paid the attorney 50 percent of her total fees to get the filings done because I was not a Texas resident. She would then call me later with a court date to go before a judge and be granted my mother's estate executrix and given a Letters of Testamentary. The Letter of Testamentary is a document that provides an executor with the power to act in a fiduciary manner on behalf of the estate. I would need to make several copies of the Letter of Testamentary to show my mother's creditors, banks, mortgage company, etc., so I could act on her behalf and handle her affairs.

Also, all my mother's belongings that were designated to be sold became part of an estate sale. An estate sale or estate liquidation is a sale to dispose of a substantial portion of the materials owned by a person who is recently deceased or who must dispose of their personal property to facilitate a move. The money from the sale went toward paying off my mother's creditors and keeping the utilities on until the house sold. I wasn't required to pay any of my mom's debt out of my wallet, but her estate was responsible for settling the debts of her creditors.

I flew back to North Carolina during the time of the estate sale. I couldn't stand to see the items my mother held dear be picked over and sold to strangers. Ironically, my mother loved a sale and meticulously took her time going through endless sales racks in discounted clothing, shoes, and home goods stores. Each item sold had a story my mother could tell; however, she was no longer with me to share it.

After the estate sale, I returned to Houston in time for probate court and stayed at my mother's house one last time before I placed the house for sale. As I walked through my mother's front door, it resonated with me that this was no longer a home but a house. The heart of that home no longer lived there; she had moved to a heavenly address. The foyer table, which displayed her grandchildren through various stages of her life, was no longer at the front door. Only one couch was left, which my mother used to lay on when she iced her knee and watched TV. The fridge and freezer that housed the vegetables and herbs she harvested from her garden were gone. The pantry was bare as well. I would never again see my mother go into the refrigerator or pantry to get ingredients to cook my favorite Trinidadian meals.

I went through the rest of the paperwork left for me to either keep or throw out, and then I went to bed to be ready to face probate court the next day.

I am vastly familiar with the uneasy feeling of appearing in family court, but sitting in probate court was a first for me. That court had a distinct energy. I sat among a group of people inside the courtroom, individually waiting to be heard by the probate judge. An attorney represented each person present, and we all shared one commonality: We had all suffered the loss of a loved one. As strangers, we sat in a collective atmosphere of pain and mourning. I sat next to my attorney and listened to the judge as he read each obituary of the dearly departed and gracefully gave condolences to each family member who approached. Several of us could not hold back our tears as we sat and waited for our turn.

Eventually, the judge approved my role as the executor of my mother's estate. My mother made this part of the process a smooth transition because her wishes were well documented in her will. However, I realized I did not have a will or an estate plan. What would my husband and children do in the event of my untimely death? What if my husband and I both died? Who would take care of our youngest son? I developed a new perspective about my own mortality in a way I'd never had before my mother's death.

Probate court made me realize I, too, needed to get my business affairs in order in the event of my death.

In Spring 2021, my husband and I obtained an attorney and put together our estate plan. We also created a trust for our children to eliminate the need to go through probate. I can only imagine how much more difficult things would have been if my mother had not had an estate plan and will. I strongly encourage you to hire an attorney to learn about the probate laws in your state and estate planning in general, including what happens to your children, assets, businesses, etc., upon your death[3].

When I returned from the probate court, the house was dead silent. There wasn't any white noise from the TV, refrigerator, or chatter from friends stopping by to visit my mom. I was left alone with thoughts of my mother's death. I struggled to sleep in the silence, knowing my mom would not be pulling into the garage and walking into the house to tell me about her day.

My insomnia led me to pray to God for comfort in my affliction and a peaceful night's rest. Before I attempted to fall asleep again, I wrote my thoughts and feelings in the journal I had been keeping since my mom's diagnosis. I woke up the next morning refreshed. That was the best sleep I'd had in a long time.

Before leaving my mother's house for the last time, I walked through every room and thanked God for all the memories we shared there and what that house meant to her. I laughed and cried at the recollection of each memory. I then stepped outside to take one last look at the garden my mother adored. The backyard was now overgrown, barren, and no longer bore fruit. It was as if my mother's cherished garden also mourned the loss of its caregiver. Sadness overwhelmed me because I would never be able to sit at the dining table and eat, laugh, and talk with my mother in her home again.

I decided to turn my sadness into purpose. I walked through each room again, but this time, I prayed for the new homeowners. I prayed that whoever bought that home would experience the warmth, love, and peace that I felt, just as everyone else did when they entered my mother's house. My mother always had a way of making everyone feel welcomed upon entering. She always offered a meal, a story, and there was always laughter. I prayed that the new homeowners would feel the energy of my loving mother in their new home. Even after death, my mother's servant heart lived on. We donated all the items that weren't purchased to her beloved Sagemont Church for people in need, just as my mom would have wanted it.

Before I left for the airport, I stopped at my mother's grave. Agony struck me as I pulled into the cemetery. I couldn't stop crying; it was surreal for me to visit my mother's grave for the first time after her funeral. The cemetery was massive, so I got lost trying to find the correct steps to my mother's burial plot. I panicked and began to cry uncontrollably. After I drove around the cemetery twice, I stumbled upon the steps and saw the pergola at the top of the hill. I parked the car as my tears continued to flow.

As I reached the top of the stairs, my tears turned to laughter. My dad had signed the paperwork for my mom to be buried on the plot, but he never changed the tombstone. I couldn't believe it! My parents' names were both on the headstone, but there was no end date for my dad. This crazy mix-up gave me a laugh and helped me to dry my tears. Not even a divorce could separate my parents from being together on a tombstone!

When I arrived back in North Carolina, I began handling my mother's business affairs on her behalf with the Letters of Testamentary in hand. It had only been a little over a month since we'd buried her. As I continued to grieve, I made phone calls to all of her creditors and banks to close her accounts. The hardest part of being an executor was repeatedly saying, "My mother passed away," as I contacted everyone she did business with to close her account. It is extremely hard to grieve as you handle an executor's responsibilities because they are a constant reminder of your loss, the reason you're calling.

Many of the businesses I called offered their condolences and were well aware of how to close out an account when someone dies. However, one company, in particular, asked to speak to my mother to close the account. It disgusted me. Active listening is so essential when you are in customer service. It only added to my pain to repeat the words, "My mother is dead," to the call agent for her to understand what was needed.

When it came to selling my mother's home, I reached out to the same friend who had been an executrix of her grandparents' estate. She was also a real estate agent, and I trusted her to help me sell my mother's home while I was in North Carolina. The house was on the market for less than two weeks and sold right before the COVID-19 pandemic hit the United States in 2020. The timing of the sale could not have been any better. Thankfully, the money earned from the estate sale and the sale of my mother's home paid off all the debts to her creditors.

I could finally rest easy that I had handled my mother's business affairs. I felt accomplished and satisfied knowing that I had followed my mother's Last Will and Testament orders. I knew my mother would be proud of me, and I realized she'd had faith in me all along to handle her affairs while she was celebrating in heaven. I just had to believe I could do it. I also kept the faith that God was guiding me throughout the entire process. God's word reminds me that He will never leave or forsake me, and I thank God that His promises never return void.

> *The Lord himself goes before you and will be with you; he will never leave you nor forsake you. Do not be afraid; do not be discouraged.*
>
> (Deuteronomy 31:8, NIV)

Now that my executrix duties were complete, I could give myself space to grieve and read the collection of thirteen journals my mother left behind.

Part 2

In Her Own Words

And then God answered: "Write this. Write what you see. Write it out in big block letters so that it can be read on the run. This vision-message is a witness pointing to what's coming. It aches for the coming—it can hardly wait! And it doesn't lie. If it seems slow in coming, wait. It's on its way. It will come right on time.

(Habakkuk 2:2-3, MSG)

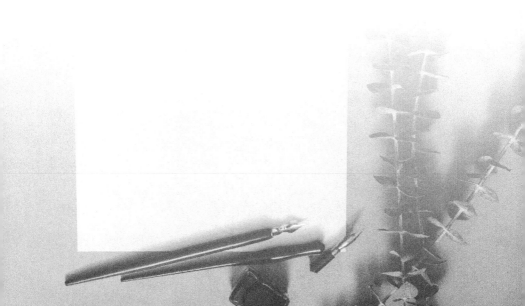

Chapter 5

Let the Journey Begin

To my surprise, while I was packing up my mother's home, I found dresser drawers full of her journals. My mother's handwritten words mean so much to me because they represent her pouring her heart onto each page. Those journals couldn't be replaced, so I made sure to pack them all in a suitcase and take them with me to North Carolina.

Once I got back home, I placed my mother's journals in chronological order because I wanted to read them as one story. I wanted to drill down and discover the parts of her I never knew. As I read each page, I allowed her words to draw me in since I could no longer physically fold into her arms like a little girl the way I'd done when she was alive.

I knew my mom was a prayer warrior before reading her journals, but the lengths to which she would pour out her heart to God amazed me. Each page of her journal contained earnest prayers for others, acknowledgment of those answered prayers, and a complete surrender to God for the prayers left unanswered. In the midst of it all, she always kept a heart of thanksgiving.

On Sunday, March 2004, my mom followed her heart's desire and began recording her daily activities in a journal. She sought God for direction on how to proceed.

There is where I found this book. I looked at it and wondered what I should do. I see this was from the past. After giving it thought, I decided to start recording my day's activity. Please, God, help me. I always wanted to do this.

My mother was born and raised in the Caribbean on the islands of Trinidad and Tobago. She left Trinidad in her late twenties on a student visa to attend cosmetology school in New York City. She never returned to her home country. Instead, she bounced around between family members who already lived in New York City to live out her American dream with her cosmetology license in hand. Unfortunately, her naivete made her a target, causing her to be taken advantage of by the people she trusted most. I don't believe my mother ever recovered from the pitfalls and traps she fell into as an immigrant to the United States. She would constantly call herself dumb for not knowing what she thought she should know. In my opinion, she never forgave herself for what she believed she had to do to survive.

Often, my mother reminded me that she didn't complete elementary school. As the oldest of ten siblings, she had to help take care of her younger brothers and sisters. She understood the value of an education because of the financial hardships she faced in her youth. She wanted me to graduate from college because regardless of the obstacles I faced, no one could take my education away.

My mom was apprehensive about her penmanship and how to tackle the latest electronics. However, despite her difficulties, she received an associate degree in Clinical Nutrition from San Jacinto Community College in Pasadena, Texas. She was so proud of her accomplishment and how far she had come. I find it mind-boggling that she shied away from writing her story of triumph and the obstacles she overcame in her lifetime.

For example, I recall my mom wanting to learn how to send text messages so she could send encouraging words and her favorite Bible verses to her grandchildren. During a visit to Texas, she asked me to show her how to create and send a text. I wrote a step-by-step process for her to follow, but she could not get the hang of it. I believe it was more fear of the technology and thinking she could not grasp the concept that stopped her, rather than her inability to learn. She ended up going "old school" and called her grandsons to speak with them on the phone instead.

After she passed away, I kept my mother's phone and went through her text messages. I found several incomplete ones and multiple messages that she had received without sending a response. My mother's attempts to text put a smile on my face because I don't think she realized how close she came to sending them correctly. All she had to do was finish her sentence and click send.

Chapter 6

Trials and Tribulations

*Consider it pure joy, my brothers and sisters, whenever you face
trials of many kinds, because you know that the testing of your
faith produces perseverance. Let perseverance finish its work so
that you may be mature and complete, not lacking anything. If
any of you lacks wisdom, you should ask God, who gives gener-
ously to all without finding fault, and it will be given to you.*

(James 1:2-5, NIV)

On Friday, March 14th, 2003, my parents divorced after being married
for 30 years. I was 27 years old and lived with my own family in Durham,
North Carolina, at the time of the divorce proceedings, and the little girl
in me wished it had happened at least 20 years earlier. I was overjoyed
when my mother finally got out of her toxic marriage. Growing up with my
parents was like being unable to wake up from an emotional nightmare.
Their marriage was tumultuous and riddled with psychological [1] and verbal abuse. Much of the trauma I experienced as a child directly correlated
to how my parents interacted and communicated.

My mother journals her experience leaving divorce court as a free woman on March 14th, 2003:

> I do not know or remember her name; it was on the bench. I was…I really do not know how I was feeling. Glad the day had finally come. I was sad because this should not have happened. Chris' lawyer was very nice. He took my hands, gave me a hug, and said, "You can start a new life now." I hugged Christine, and Becky hugged me. We spoke for a while in the hallway. Christine said they would call me. When Becky, Gabbie, and I went outside, the sun was bright. At this point, I would still say I don't know how I was feeling. All I could say is, "Thank you, Jesus."

I never knew my parents' love story or why they stayed together for so long when it was obvious they were unhappy. I only knew that a dense, dark fog of tension hung over our home. I learned how to read the room and pick up on my parents' energy at an early age, which guided how I moved throughout my home. To survive, I played outside from sunup to sundown.

When I was outdoors, I played with my friends and could be as creative as I wanted to be without dealing with the criticism of my parents. I also loved going over to my friends' houses to play. Being in someone else's home was another escape from the misery I felt at my house. I avoided having friends over because my parents couldn't hide their dysfunction if anyone came to visit. My father stayed in a bad mood. He rarely smiled unless he was watching something funny on TV. My mom was always warm and inviting toward anyone she met in public, but she couldn't be as hospitable as she wanted to be when my dad was home. As a result, we didn't have many guests unless my aunts, uncles, and cousins came to visit from Trinidad.

My mother rarely expressed to me how she truly felt. It wasn't until I read her journal entry that I came to understand she felt the same way as me. She didn't want to go home, either.

> This day I sum up as a sad sweet day.
> ① After putting all these years in the
> marriage, hoping when the children leave
> things will get better. also I was
> hoping after his serious illness.
> And pulling my self into debt to make
> the house look homely.
> ② Sweet - No more having to listen to
> the cursing, looking at me as though
> I was his worst Enemy. Would not
> even answer when I say good morning
> No more wondering what mood he.
> would be when I walk in the house
> No more Feeling I wish I did not have
> to go home.
> No more Not being able to use the
> Kitchen. as I wanted.
> Not want to eat any thing & leave
> open in the Fridge.

This day, I sum up as a sad, sweet day. 1. Sad - After putting all these years in the marriage, hoping when the children left, things would get better.

43

Also, hoping things would get better after his serious illness and putting myself into debt to make the house look homely. 2. Sweet - No more having to listen to the cursing, looking at me as though I was his worst enemy. He would not even answer when I would say, "Good Morning." No more wondering what mood he would be in when I walked in the house. No more feeling like I wished I did not have to go home. No more not being able to use the kitchen as I wanted or not wanting to eat anything that I left open in the fridge.

I also endured watching my parents give each other the silent treatment for months on end until the holiday season arrived. For some weird reason, my parents smiled and laughed during the holidays as if they liked each other again. It was so emotionally confusing to me because they never resolved their anger or talked through why they stopped talking to each other in the first place. And just like clockwork, after the holidays, they stopped talking to each other or would argue over the stupidest things. I never understood why my mom stayed in a marriage that did not nurture or foster growth. My parents' marriage resembled a stagnant pool of water that was unsafe to drink.

For years, I felt resentful toward my mom for staying in an unhealthy relationship, but for some reason, I did not hold this same resentment toward my father. I'm not sure if it is because I was scared of him, just like my mother, or the fact that he directly took his anger out on her most of the time instead of me. Although I never saw my father physically strike my mother, I understood her fears and anxiety on a more personal level through her journal writings:

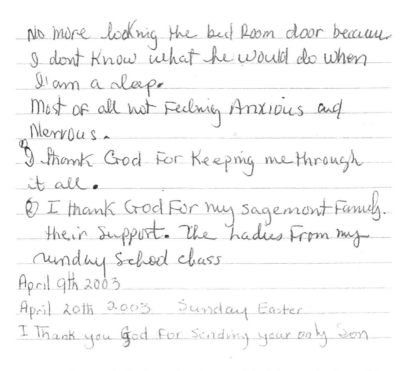

No more locking the bedroom door because I don't know what he would do when I am asleep. 1. Most of all, not feeling anxious and nervous. I thank God for keeping me through it all. 2. I thank God for my Sagemont Family and their support. Also, the ladies from my Sunday School class.

My mother was passive-aggressive and would badmouth my father to me as if I was her girlfriend. She would remind me how my father pushed her while pregnant with me, and she bore the scar on her forehead to prove it. She even went as far as telling me he wanted her to abort me and still had the paperwork to prove it. I had no idea how to process that information. When my mother told me how evil my father was, I internalized it to mean that I was half-evil. I bore many similar emotional scars from all of their inter-fighting and turmoil.

However, I found myself in the same position as my parents in my late twenties. I continued the dysfunctional cycle. Ironically, I resented my mother for staying in an unhealthy relationship with my father for 30 years, but I stayed in an unhealthy relationship for 11 years, which negatively affected my two older sons. I realized I was no different than my mom.

Chapter 7

Control-Alt-Delete

Ctrl-Alt-Del: First used to reboot DOS PCs, the keystrokes were chosen by IBM in 1981. The key combination in Windows that enables a user to terminate an unresponsive application. When all three keys are pressed at the same time, the Task Manager utility is launched, which displays all open applications. It also enables the user to shut down the computer.[1]

I have worked in the information technology industry for over 20 years. My career began as an IT analyst working at a call center for a Fortune 500 company. When customers complained about their applications or PC freezing, we would tell them to press Control-Alt-Delete to reboot their entire system and start over—rebooting solved most of our customers' problems. In the same way, if something is not working for you in life, you can reboot as many times as necessary. Think of each reboot as a new chapter in your life. It may be scary to start over, but if you don't, you can become frozen, paralyzed with fear, and unable to move forward.

My mother's Control-Alt-Delete reboot came in three stages: a divorce, a new home, and retirement. After her divorce, my mom began to live life on her terms. Based on what I've read in my mother's journals, she stayed at several family and friends' homes when she moved out of the house she shared with my dad. I learned so much about my mother's story from her writings.

During that time in her life, she periodically called and assured me that she was safe, but the truth was, she kept a lot from me. I know she wanted to keep me from worrying about her, but I could tell she was concerned about her next steps. Still, in my heart, I knew things would work out for my mother as long as she had faith, hope, and determination to succeed. I don't know where to gauge her faith meter, but she courageously moved forward despite her fears, and she should have felt proud of herself. I was just happy she finally stepped out on her own and removed herself from such a toxic environment.

I dealt with my own separation (in the form of an annulment) after 11 years of marriage, so I could relate to how my mother felt when I read what she had written after her divorce. A divorce/separation often leads to a transitional phase where many thoughts run through your head. For example, will you have enough money to survive on your own? How will you celebrate holidays and birthdays? Who do you call when you have an emergency? You also have to deal with the emotional distress of transporting children on alternating weekends and holidays.

However, there can be silver linings as well. During a reboot, you get to decide for yourself how your new life will look. My mother reflected on the highs and lows of her transitional period at the end of December 2003.

December 2003 - This year I will be in Houston
Not North Carolina.
I working all week. 12/22 - 12/26.
This year is Kind of happy and sad -
(A) Expecting my New home is exciting,
(B) Not having or being with the children is sad.
But I believe God is in Control and Know why it
it is happening.
I'm waiting for God to Show me.
I work Christmas day. I was OK stay on the Job late.
Came in 9pm staying at Colony Renting a Rm.
took a Shower, She had some friends Come over. I visit
with them a while and went to bed.
I do have a lot to thank God for.

December 2003: This year, I will be in Houston, not North Carolina. I am working all week—12/22–12/26. This year is kind of happy and sad:

A. Expecting my new home is exciting.
B. Not having or being with the children is sad.

But I believe God is in control and knows why it is happening. I am waiting for God to show me. I work Christmas Day. I was okay staying on the job late. I'm staying at Gloria's renting a room. I took a shower. She had some friends come over. I visited with them for a while and went to bed. I do have a lot to thank God for.

In December of 2003, I was married with a three-year-old and a three-month-old. My mother anticipated visiting my family and me every Christmas. She loved spending time with her grandchildren, and I loved having her as well. She would help me out with the laundry, cooking, cleaning, and taking care of the boys. My husband at the time would work 12-hour shifts on the weekend, so I didn't have a moment to breathe with two children under the age of three. I counted down the days to my mother's visits because I could finally get some rest.

Unfortunately, she had to work that year, so we didn't get to spend Christmas together. Hospitals don't close. As a clinician dietician for MD

Anderson Cancer Center, she had to put in for time off before anyone else on her team, and that year, one of her co-workers beat her to taking time off during the Christmas holidays. My mother was distraught by this, but I reassured her that we would see her after Christmas, and it would be okay.

My mother's second reboot resulted in homeownership. It was a hard pill to swallow for my mother not to get time off work to spend with my family and me for Christmas. However, in March 2004, she closed on her own home. She entered the new year with a new house in her name! Now my mom could entertain guests, grow her own fruits and vegetables, and come in and out of her home as she pleased. Glory be to God!

My mom endured such heartache living with my dad and shuffling between friends and family after the divorce. After her death, I couldn't help but notice that her bedroom was the only room in the house with a lock and key. She also had a pole behind her bedroom door that she used as a barricade preventing anyone from entering if they got past the locked door. It was a heartbreaking realization for me because not even a new home could not erase the unhealed trauma from her previous relationship.

The third reboot was retirement. For as long as I could remember, my mother got up at 4:00 a.m. to get ready for work. She had to give herself enough time to get ready for work and drive through downtown Houston traffic. She was the first person out of the house every morning, then me, and then my dad. My mom was tired when she came home from the hospital because she spent all day on her feet visiting patients. Often, she told me to cook side dishes for dinner while she cooked whatever protein she had on hand. She worked like that every day for over 26 years until her retirement.

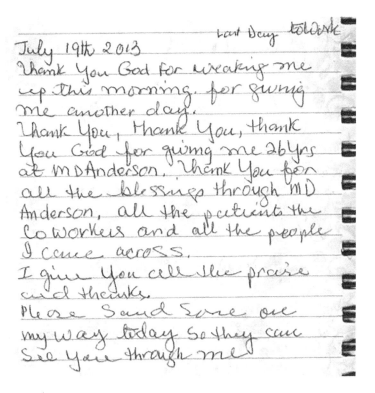

July 19th, 2013 - Last Day to Work

Thank you for waking me up this morning, for giving me another day. Thank you, thank you, thank you, God, for giving me 26 years at MD Anderson. Thank you for all the blessings through MD Anderson, all the patients, the co-workers, and the people I came across. I give you all the praise and thanks. Please send someone my way today so they can see you through me.

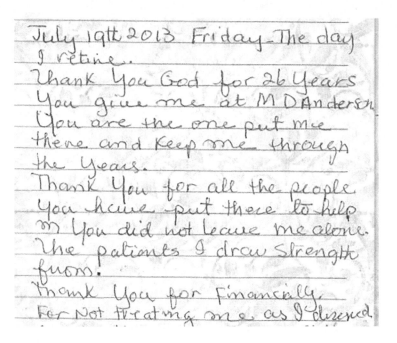

July 19th, 2013 - Friday - The Day I Retire

Thank you, God, for the 26 years you gave me at MD Anderson. You are the one who put me there and kept me through the years. Thank you for all the people you have put there to help on. You did not leave me alone. The patients I draw strength from. Thank you for financially providing, for not treating me as I deserved.

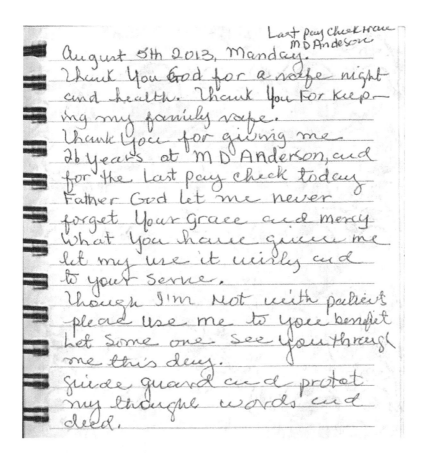

August 5th, 2013, Monday - Last Paycheck from MD Anderson

Thank you, God, for a safe night and health. Thank you for keeping my family safe. Thank you for giving me 26 years at MD Anderson and the last paycheck today. Father God, let me never forget your grace and mercy. What you have given me, let me use it wisely and to your service. Though I am not with patients, please use me to your benefit. Let someone see you through me this day. Guide, guard, and protect my thoughts, words, and deeds.

My mother was so grateful for the opportunities MD Anderson provided to her. I still remember all the hard work she put in, which led to her last day at work. I remember her studying for her associate degree to become a clinical dietician. I remember my mother doing clinical rotations at schools in order to learn about and understand children's nutrition. She even worked as a lunch lady for the day at a local school. She told me she tried to get the pizza into a triangle, but the lunch ladies said it had to be a rectangle to fit the lunch tray. I laughed so hard at the story because clearly, my mother had never seen a public-school lunch.

After her death, I found many pictures from her college graduation. I was a young girl in elementary school smiling right there in pictures with her. I do not remember that moment captured in time, but I appreciate the photos that captured those milestones in my mother's life. I also remember visiting my mother at her job while she was still on the clock. She was always so happy to show me around to all her co-workers and doctors. I was embarrassed, but my mother seemed to enjoy having those proud mom moments.

The beauty of using Control-Alt-Delete is that you can reboot as many times as needed. The end of one chapter is the beginning of another, and the rest of the story is yet to be written. My mother's Control-Alt-Delete stories taught me about her ability to overcome and persevere through life's difficulties and challenges. The summer before she passed away, my mother told me that she was proud of me for all that I had overcome and that I was still standing, despite my own challenges. I wish I had known half of what was in her journals while she was alive because I could have expressed how proud I was of her before she passed away. I often wonder if knowing her story would have prevented me from making some of my life decisions. However, I cannot harp on what-ifs. Instead, I choose to give myself permission to reboot as many times as necessary and keep turning the page to a new chapter each time.

Chapter 8

P.U.S.H.: Pray Until Something Happens

Throughout my life, I have had difficulty regulating my emotions. At times, a negative emotion would camp out in my brain, and I would end up in a never-ending spiral of emotions. My first call would often be to my mother for reassurance, but she always seemed quick to get off the phone. I didn't know what to think about that. Did she care? Was she incapable of processing my circumstances? What I eventually realized is that my mother got off the phone and prayed. She also wrote out her prayers in her journals. Each journal consisted of handwritten words that described my mother's thoughts, daily activities, and prayers.

My mother embodied the acronym PUSH; she continuously "prayed until something happened." There is something to be said about the persistent prayers of a mother or grandmother. I feel my mother's spirit near me after her death when I read through her journaled prayers. I loved reading her vulnerability and complete surrender to God. On March 29th, 2015, she eloquently prayed to the God of Peace, asking for strength to relinquish the fear that had consumed her for most of her life. So much of childhood revolved around my mother parenting me from a state of fear. It was beautiful to read that a level of self-awareness awakened in her spirit, prompting her to release the grip that fear had on her mind for all these years.

Sunday, March 29th, 2015

Thank you, God, for a safe night and a beautiful Sunday. Thank you for all your blessings. Thank you for Sagemont Church, Brother John, and all the family members. Thank you for the good start of Holy Week and the special program. I pray this week will bear the fruit of salvation, and I will see many saved. Dear God, work on me. Remove all the thoughts and fear in me, which have had a hold on me most of my life. Please remove them. I want to put you first.

My mother continuously gave God praise for her church family and all the good works her church did to expand the kingdom of God. There is a beautiful, vulnerable moment where my mom realized fear had taken her thoughts captive for most of her life. She pleaded to God, asking Him to help renew her mind to allow His voice to be louder than her fears. My mom was ready to release fear so she could walk boldly with God.

My mother lived out this verse in Romans 12:2 (NIV):

> *Do not conform to the pattern of this world but be transformed by the renewing of your mind. Then you will be able to test and approve what God's will is—his good, pleasing, and perfect will.*

My spiritual walk and life experiences have taught me that God's purpose will come to fruition regardless of our life circumstances; His will cannot be denied. I am living proof! I grappled with depression for decades due to my childhood, the unforeseen and abrupt end of my first marriage, unemployment, life as a single mom, and becoming pregnant with another child while unemployed. All of these events took a toll on me. I went from one traumatic event to the next without processing any of them.

At one point, I was prescribed 150mg of Sertraline. I lost hope because I felt I had brought shame upon myself because of my poor decisions. I spent a lot of time sleeping to ignore my circumstances. I got out of bed for the sake of taking care of my children, but not for myself. Life seemed hopeless, and no amount of Sertraline seemed to help. I managed to get by because of an obligation to my family, but not because I wanted to live.

Taking my life was not a viable option because I didn't want to cause my children any more pain. Instead, I pushed my pain down to survive and coasted through life. Unfortunately, all I was doing was killing my spirit by not dealing with the unresolved trauma.

Seeing my mother's last breath in a hospice facility was a wake-up call. During prayer, I felt God speaking directly to me and asking me, "How do you want to live out the remaining time you have on earth?" That question made me recognize that I had been merely surviving in life up until that point. Now, I wanted to flourish and thrive.

Prayers for Her Children and Grandchildren

My mother journaled her intercessory prayers for her family and friends. I always knew she was a praying woman, but I wasn't aware of the depths of her prayers and how she came before God, interceding on behalf of her family, friends, and everyone she encountered, until I read her journals.

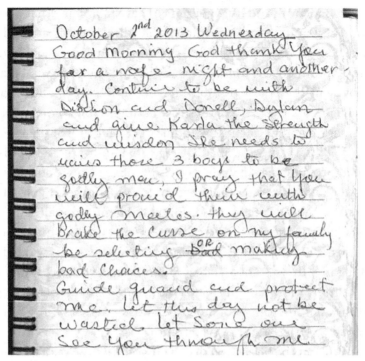

Wednesday, October 2nd, 2013

Good morning. God. Thank you for a safe night and another day. Continue to be with Dischon, Dorell, and Dylan, and give Karla the strength and wisdom she needs to raise those three boys to be godly men. I pray that you will provide them with godly mates. They will break the curse on my family of selecting or making bad choices. Guide, guard, and protect me. Let this day not be wasted. Let someone see you through me.

My mother believed our family suffered from a generational curse concerning relationships and marriage. First, there was my grandmother (she never married and had ten children), then my mother's two marriages ended in divorce, and finally, my marriage of 11 years ended in an annulment. That makes three generations of not hitting the marriage department out of the park. However, I learned a different perspective about generational curses through cognitive behavior therapy. I believe that the underlying source of my family's generational curse is unhealed trauma. We must reveal unhealed trauma in order for the healing process to take root in our lives. When we suffer in silence, we hear, think, and feel differently than when we are healed. Some behaviors rooted in unsolved trauma show up as anger, guilt, depression, and shame. We make decisions based on these unregulated emotions coupled with unhealed trauma, and then we experience even more heartache and pain.

Despite the trauma she endured, the love my mother had for her children and grandchildren was undeniable. She never stopped praying for us, and she dedicated herself to fulfilling her role as a mother and grandmother. At the end of the day, we were so blessed to receive all her love and kindness.

Praying Through the Pain

February 24th, 2014 was the first journal entry when my mom spoke about her back pain, which was a symptom of what would eventually end her life five years later: Primary CNS melanoma. My mom did not ask God why she experienced pain. Instead, she asked, "What lesson are you teaching me?" It was a profound question. I want to be positive and believe my mother was looking at her pain through the lens of faith. However, after reading her journals, I learned my mother lived with a lot of guilt, shame, and resentment about her condition. She seemed to think God was inflicting pain to teach her a lesson for her decisions throughout her life. I remember coming out of a difficult situation while pregnant with my third son and finally got a job after a year of searching. My mother was happy for me but ended the conversation by saying, "Don't do anything to make God mad." Her statement confused me at the time, but now I understand that she lived with religious guilt.

During my spiritual journey in bible study, I have learned that there is a big difference between the emotions of conviction and shame. Conviction tells us that our *actions* are wrong, and it alerts us to correct our mistakes and learn from them. Shame, however, is an attack on our identity; it tells us *we* are inadequate. The enemy uses shame to keep us in a cycle of condemnation and isolation, leading to depression. Shame convinces us that God is mad at us and we have messed up too much to fulfill our potential, which is a lie! Jesus came to free us from the burden of shame and give us a new identity![1]

> *Therefore, there is now no condemnation for those who are in Christ Jesus.*
>
> (Romans 8:1, NIV)

Church Conference 2-9 pm

Febuary 24th 2014 monday
Thank You God for giving me
one more day. for health.
for family, friends, Sagemont
Church. For America
Thank You for being with
Dischon and Donell. I pray
they will be great and
mighty me through You. their
hears will be focus on you.
Dear God what are You trying
to teach me through Back pain
be with me guide, guard

and protect my thoughts words
and deeds. let some one
see You through me.
Be with me this day
let me be a good representation
of You today. please ease the
pain so I can do what ever
tasks is assigned to me
with out problems.

Monday, February 24th, 2014

Thank you, God, for giving me one more day for health, for family, friends, Sagemont Church, and for America. Thank you for being with Dischon and Dorell. I pray they will be great mighty men through you, and their hearts will be focused on you. Dear God, what are you trying to teach me through the back pain? Be with me, guide, guard, and protect me through my thoughts, words, and deeds. Let someone see you through me. Be with me today. Let me be a good representation of you today. Please ease the pain so I can do whatever task is assigned to me without problems.

Prayers of Gratitude

On December 7th, 2016, an 18-wheeler hit my mother as she was driving home. Thank God she survived. It felt like an electric shock went through my body when I heard the news. When I spoke with her on the phone, she reassured me in her typical fashion that she was fine and praised God for sparing her life. She then described having an out-of-body experience, seeing herself hovering above her car looking down at the multi-vehicle collision after being hit. I wish I could personally thank the firefighter who pried my mother out of her car, which was crushed against the guardrail on the highway. Nevertheless, I give the Almighty God the praise.

I truly admire my mother for not allowing the accident to prevent her from moving forward. I would have been fearful of driving again after going through such a traumatic experience, but my mother was fearless and ready to get back behind the wheel. She described this traumatic event in vivid detail in her journal entries a few days after it happened. Even while healing from the car accident, she continued to give God praise and prayed for others. It was a true testament to her faith.

> December 9th 2016 Wednesday
> On my way home from
> Sydney Rose. On Belt Way 8 th
> was hit by an 18 wheeler.
> Thank God for protecting me.
> Could have been badly Ingery
> or dead.
> Some thing happened do not know
> how to explain it, will try

Wednesday, December 7th, 2016

On my way home from SRW house on Beltway 8, I was hit by an 18-wheeler. Thank God for protecting me. I could have been badly injured or dead. Something happened. I do not know how to explain it; I will try.

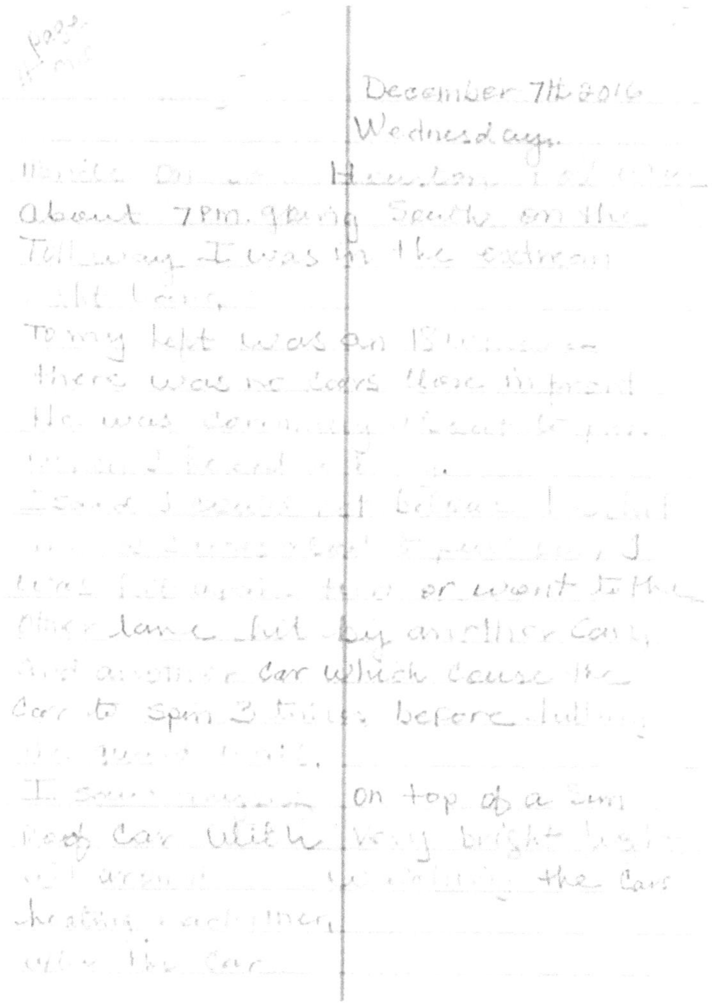

[handwritten journal entry, partially legible]

December 7th 2016
Wednesday.

About 7 p.m. going South on the
Tollway I was in the extreme
right lane.

To my left was an 18...
there was no cars close in front
He was coming...

...was put again... or went to the
other lane but by another car,
and another car which cause the
car to spin 3 times before hitting
the guardrail.

I saw... on top of a sun
roof car with very bright light
all around me watching the cars
hitting each other,
...the car

Wednesday, December 7th, 2016

Miracle on Sam Houston Tollway

About 7 p.m. going south on the Tollway, I was in the extreme right lane. To my left was an 18-wheeler. There were no cars close in front. He was coming about to pass when I heard a loud bang! I said, "I could not believe he hit me." As I was about to pull over, I was hit again. I was turned and went into the other lane, hit by a car and then another car, which caused the car to spin three times before hitting the guardrail. I saw myself on top of the sunroof with very bright light all around me, watching the cars hit each other.

When my mother told me about her out-of-body experience, I was in shock. Tears rolled down my cheeks because it hit me in my gut that I could have lost my mother in a horrific way. I'd heard about out-of-body experience stories on television, but I wasn't sure whether or not I believed in them. However, my mother's experience brought the idea a little too close to home. She convinced me that it wasn't farfetched to have a supernatural experience.

Thursday, December 8th, 2016

Good morning, God. Thank you for a safe night and for sparing my life to see another day. I can walk and talk. Thank you, God. Thank you, thank you, thank you for sparing my life. Show me your will for me this day. I need your guidance today. There is so much that needs to be done. Please guide me. Show me what you want me to do. Be with me, hold my hands, and walk with me. Guide, guard, and protect my thoughts, words, and deeds. I thank you for America.

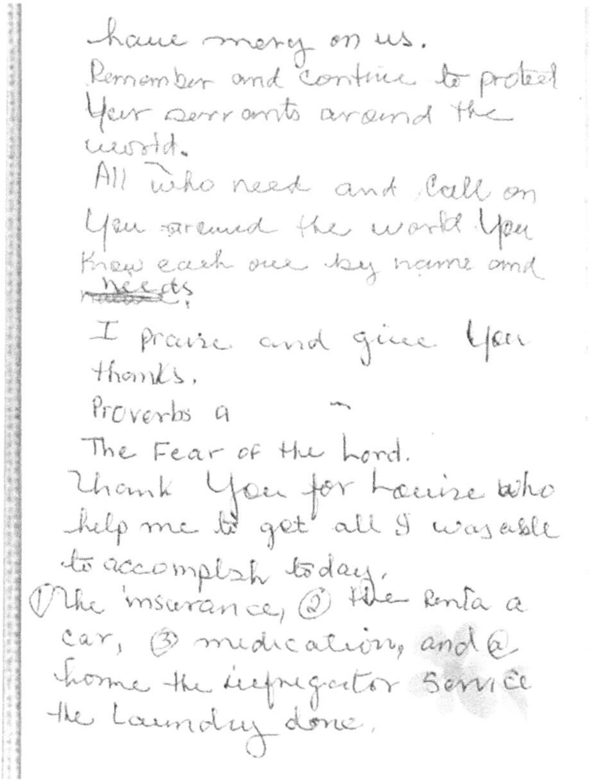

[Handwritten journal entry]

> have mercy on us.
> Remember and continue to protect
> Your servants around the
> world.
> All who need and call on
> You around the world You
> know each one by name and
> needs.
> I praise and give You
> thanks.
> Proverbs 9
> The Fear of the Lord.
> Thank You for Louise who
> help me to get all I was able
> to accomplish today.
> ① The insurance, ② the Rental a
> car, ③ medication, and ④
> home the refrigerator service
> the Laundry done.

Have mercy on us. Remember and continue to protect your servants around the world, all who need and call on you around the world. You know each one by name and their needs. I praise and give you thanks. Proverbs 9. The Fear of the Lord. Thank you for Louise, who helped me to get all I was able to accomplish today. 1. Insurance, 2. Rental car, 3. Medication and at-home refrigerator service and the laundry done.

I sent a care package to my mom after the car accident, which included a journal for her to write out her thoughts. I wrote an encouraging message inside the journal to keep her motivated. To my surprise, when I found this journal, I saw where my mother had replied to my message. Reading her words after her death gave me the feeling that she was still communicating with me. At the same time, in the process of transcribing my message to my mother, I realized I needed to take my own advice.

Mommy, thank you for all that you do! You truly are a blessing! I thank God your life was spared—it wasn't your time! Life has just begun for you—may you continue to live each day to the fullest! Never look back, do not fear, and remember God is in control and has the final say! I love you! Love, Karla.

Thank you, Karla. I pray God will show me His will for me and why he spared my life. December 7th, 2016, Beltway 8 or Sam Houston Tollway.

Over time, my mother continued to give God, her protector, the praise for sparing her life and continued to pray for others worldwide. Her faith never wavered as a result of the accident. God gave my mother another chance at life, and she did not squander it. She did not know what was next for her, but she asked God to order her steps, hold her hand, and guide her. She completely surrendered to God's plan for her life. My mother's ability to trust God despite her circumstances evoked Proverbs 3:5-6 (NIV):

> *Trust in the Lord with all your heart and lean not on your own understanding; in all your ways, submit to him, and he will make your paths straight.*

PRAYERS FOR DIRECTION

On May 31st, 2017, my mother attended the funeral of her pastor's wife. She never let a moment go by without leaning into what the Holy Spirit communicated to her. At the funeral, she had a moment of reflection where she asked for God's direction about reaching young people and teaching them about the gift of salvation. I don't believe my mother realized she had already been spreading the good news of Jesus all along to all who would listen.

Dentist, Bank,
Mrs Beath Morgan Service.
Got there at 4.00pm leave the
Church at 8.18pm. Was a
beautiful Service the children
and grandchildren spoke and
Read the present Scriptures
A beautiful scriptures was there
of her from child hood to her
Last days.
She has leave a beautiful
legracy. Went home on may
28th 2017 3:30 pm.
I glad we spoke, she called
me after sending a papaya
through Brother Stuart.
Show me Lord how I can help
Young people how beautiful
life could be when you

accept and trust the Lord.
at and early age.
It does not mean You will
not have trials, But it makes
a difference when You know
and trust the Lord.
She has leave me thinking
on how I can make a
difference in other people lives.
Help me Lord show me
how I can help.
Even though my life is
was so mess up.
lead me in the way I can
help my grandsons.
From this day Lord where You
lead I will follow.

Mrs. Beth Morgan service. I got there at 4:00 p.m. It was a beautiful service. The children and grandchildren spoke and read her favorite scriptures. Beautiful scriptures were shown from her childhood to her last days. She left a beautiful legacy. She went home on May 28th, 2017, at 3:30 p.m. I'm glad we spoke. She called me after I sent her papaya through Brother Stuart. Show me, Lord, how I can help young people see how beautiful life can be when you accept and trust the Lord at an early age. It does not mean you will not have trials, but it makes a difference when you know and trust the Lord. She has me thinking about how I can make a difference in other people's lives. Help me, Lord, show me how I can help. Even though my life was so messed up, it led me in the way that I can help my grandsons. From this day, Lord, where you lead, I will follow.

My mother reflected on how she could make a difference in other people's lives at a funeral, and I shared that same sentiment at her funeral. Self-realization set in my spirit after my mother's death. I knew I wanted to live a more purposeful life and let go of any attachments that no longer served me. I spent much of my life holding on to pain, trauma, and anger. I was merely surviving in life; I was not thriving.

Just as my mom prayed to God for direction, I also asked God to show me how to live each day intentionally. Death is imminent. How we live each day is a choice. Since my mother's death, I have been intentional and more self-aware about how I show up in this world each day. I, too, want to live and leave a legacy of love, hope, and inspiration for myself, my husband, and my children when God calls me home.

Chapter 9

Complete Surrender

Sometimes in life, you can face an obstacle so big that you realize there is nothing within your power that you can do. You are at a point of complete surrender to the authority over your life. By faith, you surrender to the uncertainty, knowing that God is bigger than any obstacle you might face.

My mother's last two journals from 2018 to 2019 spoke about the extreme pain she felt in her knees after her second knee replacement. She went through many physical therapy appointments and manipulations of her knees to help her regain full movement. She ended up needing to use a cane and a pain management plan to function. To know my mother is to know that she loved to get up and go when she pleased. It tested my mother's faith when her knees became a hindrance to her freedom, impacting her travel plans and her ability to move around in her home and garden. Despite the pain, she prayed to God for guidance, healing and had a heart of gratitude for friends, family, and all that she could still accomplish.

Dear God I come before You I need You. Show me Your will for me with my knee. I am confused. But You have the answer. IF You want to teach me some thing show me. I ask for healing if it is You will. IF Not give me what I need to accept it. I ask this in You Son's name Jesus Christ Amen

Monday, February 25th, 2019

Dear God, I come before you. I need you. Show me your will for me with my knees. I am confused. But you have the answer. If you want to teach me something, show me. I ask for healing if it is your will. If not, give me what I need to accept it. I ask this in your son's name, Jesus Christ. Amen.

I don't know if my mom noticed, but she had a verse printed at the bottom of her journal that aligned beautifully with her prayer: *"Be still, and know that I am God" (Psalm 46:10 NIV)*. There was nothing my mother could do except put her trust in God. Her pain was unbearable, but the God she served was greater than the pain she faced at that moment.

In my mother's last journal, she wrote her last words before the pain became too much for her to write out to God. My heart grew heavy as I visualized my mother becoming ravished by cancer and losing the ability to use her hands to write out her prayers. I can't imagine the pain she felt, and there was nothing she could do but surrender to it. August 27th, 2019, was her last fully written journal entry.

> August 27th 2019 Tuesday
> Good mornin my God, thank You
> for the safe night. You gave me
> my family and friends. I thank
> You for this new day, Show
> me Your will for it. Speake
> to me. Thank You for all
> Your grace and mercies.
> Be with me hold my
> hands, walk with me, guide
> guard and protect my thoughts
> words and deeds, as I make
> this appointments. Lord I put
> it in You hands.
> Father God be with those
> three boys my grand Sons.
> Thank You for America, Forgive
> us our sins.
> Remember and have mercy on
> all who need and call on
> You where ever they are
> You know each one by name
> and needs.

Tuesday, August 27th, 2019

Good morning, God. Thank you for the safe night you gave me, my family, and friends. I thank you for this day, show me your will for it. Speak to me. Thank you for all your grace and mercies. Be with me. Hold my hands, walk with me. Guide, guard, and protect my thoughts, words, and deeds as I make this appointment. Lord, I put it in your hands. Father God, be with those three boys, my grandsons. Thank you for America. Forgive us for our sins. Remember and have mercy on all who need and call on you. Wherever they are, know each one by name and needs.

The next two weeks of her journal writings left a lump in my throat. The words on the last journal pages decreased, and her handwriting became illegible. She could no longer write full pages; instead, she wrote "pain" in red ink next to her last words. She also wrote the word "verbal" at the end of each entry when she could no longer write. I can picture my mother calling out to God in complete surrender when her hands no longer had the power to write.

The handwritten words she could produce repeatedly gave God praise. She maintained her heart of gratitude, thanking God for her family and friends. Thanking God for America was a constant thread in her journal writings as well. My mother felt that her move from Trinidad and Tobago to the United States of America allowed her to live the American dream, and she was forever grateful for that. She even thanked God for the pain. Though it was unpleasant, she was still alive.

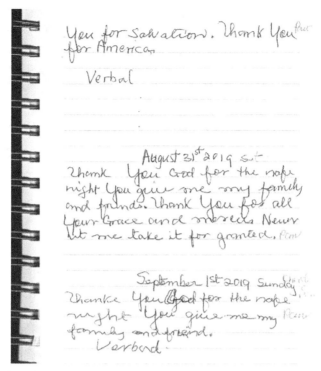

Wednesday, August 28th, 2019

Good morning, God. Thank you for the safe night you gave me, my family, and friends. (Verbal)

Thursday, August 29th, 2019 - Dr. Appt

Thank you, God, for the safe night you gave me, my family, and friends. (Verbal)

Friday, August 30th, 2019

Thank you, God, for the safe night you gave me, my family, and friends. Thank you, God, for salvation. Thank you for America. (Verbal)

Saturday, August 31st, 2019

Thank you, God, for the safe night you gave me, my family, and friends. Thank you for all your grace and mercy. Never let me take it for granted. (Pain)

Sunday, September 1st, 2019

Thank you, God, for the safe night you gave me, my family, and friends. (Verbal)

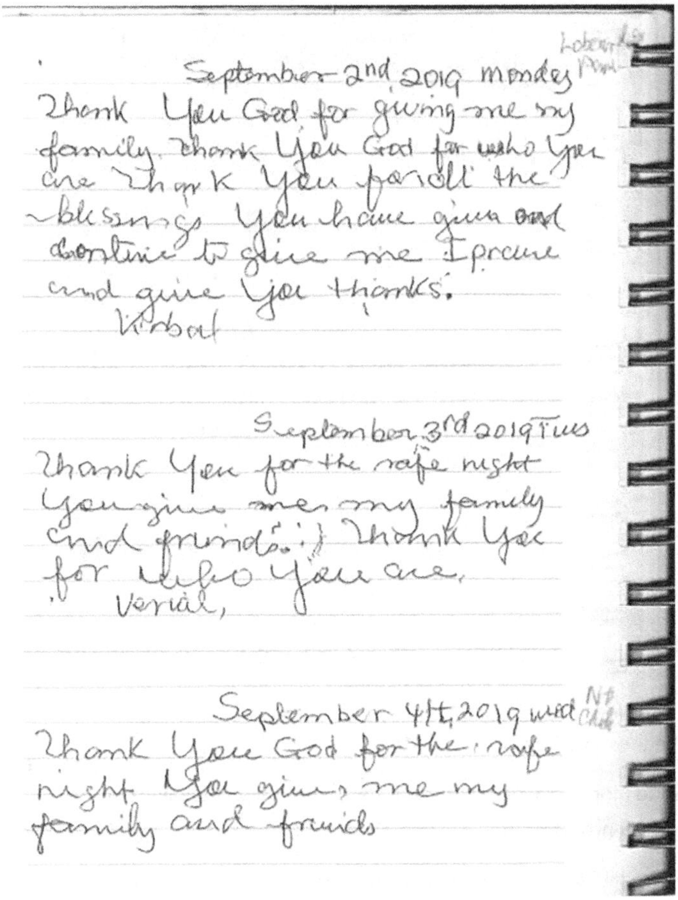

[Handwritten journal entries]

> September 2nd 2019 monday
> Thank You God for giving me my
> family. Thank You God for who You
> are. Thank You for all the
> blessings You have given and
> continue to give me. I praise
> and give You thanks.
> Verbal

> September 3rd 2019 Tues
> Thank You for the safe night
> You give me my family
> and friends. :) Thank You
> for who You are.
> Verial,

> September 4th, 2019 wed
> Thank You God for the safe
> night You gives me my
> family and friends

Monday, September 2nd, 2019 - Pain

Thank you, God, for giving me my family. Thank you, God, for who you are. Thank you for the blessings you have given and continue to give me. I praise and give you thanks. (Verbal)

Tuesday, September 3rd, 2019

Thank you for the safe night you gave me, my family, and friends. Thank you for who you are. (Verbal)

Wednesday, September 4th, 2019

Thank you, God, for the safe night you gave me, my family, and friends.

Thursday, September 5th, 2019

Thank you, God, for the safe night you gave me, my family, and friends.
I thank you for everything you have given and continue to give. (Verbal)

Friday, September 6th, 2019

Thank you for protecting me, my family, and friends. Thank you for everything, even the pain, though it is not pleasant. (Pain) (Verbal)

The page displayed above is the last one in my mother's journal, and on that day, she mustered up the strength to write her gratitude to God for her family and friends. As I sat and reflected on this page, I cried uncontrollably. Seeing the decline of her penmanship as I made my way down the page broke my heart in a thousand pieces. An influx of thoughts ran through my head. Was it too painful for her to write? Had the cancer spread throughout her body at that point? Was that when she began to lose the ability to use her hands? I tried to make sense of it all, but I couldn't turn back time.

On Sunday, September 8th, 2019, my mother wrote her last journal entry giving God the glory by simply stating, "Good morning, God!" My mother must have been in a tremendous state of pain, but that didn't stop her from giving God praise. As I read that last entry, I was in awe of my mother's faith and strength under the weight of what cancer had done to her body. At the same time, my heart ached for her because I didn't think she realized how strong she was. I hope that before she took her last breath, she recognized the essence of who she truly was and didn't dwell on the poor decisions she made in her life.

Saturday, September 7th, 2019 - Pain

Thank you, God, for protecting me, my family, and friends. Bless Jennifer for the extra help she gave me with cleaning. Louise and Karen.

Sunday, September 8th, 2019

Good Morning God.

My mother's words will continue to live on for generations to come. Her prayers and words of encouragement walk hand-in-hand with God's Living Word, which will not return to Him void. She spoke life over her family and friends, and her words continue to uplift my spirit even a year after her death. My mother left this earth to be with her Lord and Savior, leaving behind her fears and self-doubt. This truth helped me find peace in knowing that she is no longer in physical pain or struggling with the emotional turmoil of living with regret.

> *"Cancer wouldn't win if I died. Cancer would only win if I failed to cherish Jesus Christ. When people see us smile in the midst of trials, they will look at us and think, "Her God must be pretty great to inspire that kind of loyalty. I think that it's amazing that she can smile in the midst of her affliction. I want what she has. I need her joy. Oh, what a rich testimony that is."*
>
> —Joni Eareckson Tada

I thank you, Mommy, for diligently writing every day. I am so glad you left a collection of journals. When I miss you most, I can read one of your journals that are full of your sermon notes, bible verses, and prayers. Mommy, your journal writings helped me in my broken-heartedness and guided me on the journey of healing.

We serve a BIG God; therefore, our dreams and desires should be just as BIG! What started as my mom's desire to write turned into a collection of journals that are now transcribed into a book to encourage others. My mother's prayers and life experiences were not in vain; they all came together for a greater purpose than she could have ever known.

> *However, as it is written: "What no eye has seen, what no ear has heard, and what no human mind has conceived"—the things God has prepared for those who love him.*
>
> (1 Corinthians 2:9, NIV)

On Sunday, March 2004, my mother's desire aligned with God's will for her life. She started recording her daily activities and asked God to help her with her writing because it was something she always wanted to do. Fifteen years later, I can say, "Mommy, you did it!" I am so proud of you! You kept the faith until your last breath.

> *I have fought the good fight, I have finished the race, I have kept the faith.*
>
> (2 Timothy 4:7, NIV)

Part 3

Give Yourself Permission

There is a time for everything, and a season for every activity
under the heavens:
a time to be born and a time to die,
a time to plant and a time to uproot,
a time to kill and a time to heal,
a time to tear down and a time to build,
a time to weep and a time to laugh,
a time to mourn and a time to dance.

(Ecclesiastes 3:1-4 NIV)

Chapter 10

Reveal, Heal, Thrive

REVEAL THE PAIN

I had handled all business matters of my mother's estate. My mother was resting in heaven with the Lord, and I was here on earth grappling with the idea of what was next for me. I replayed different scenarios and outcomes that could have potentially prolonged my mother's life, but they were all useless; she was still gone. I wanted to make sense of her death, but I couldn't.

For weeks, I camped out in the book of Revelation in the Bible. I would spend hours reading Revelation to learn more about heaven. I wanted answers about what my mother might be experiencing in the afterlife. Did she have assigned angel duties? Was she on the hospitality committee since she had loved entertaining guests when she was alive? Was she cooking heavenly meals and desserts? Was angel food cake a thing? Was the overindulgence of chocolate considered sinful? Could you eat whatever you wanted and not get fat?

Soon, I found myself in an unhealthy emotional spiral trying to make sense of things I would not know until God called me home. I wasn't ready to die. I wanted to live in a new way, but first, I had to embrace my emotions.

For me, grief was not a linear process with a clear starting and endpoint (i.e., the Kubler-Ross Grief Cycle[1]).

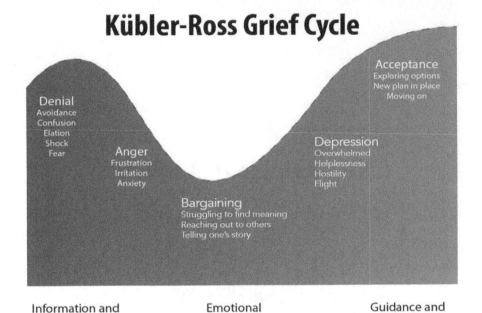

Kübler-Ross Grief Cycle

Denial
Avoidance
Confusion
Elation
Shock
Fear

Anger
Frustration
Irritation
Anxiety

Bargaining
Struggling to find meaning
Reaching out to others
Telling one's story

Depression
Overwhelmed
Helplessness
Hostility
Flight

Acceptance
Exploring options
New plan in place
Moving on

Information and
Communication

Emotional
Support

Guidance and
Direction

Instead, my grieving process was in the form of a rotating cycle of emotions. I would feel fine one minute, and then the thought of my mother triggered me, and I became a sobbing mess all over again. Grief came at me like a massive wave that knocked me down each time I tried to get up. I felt stuck in a continuous emotional loop for quite some time.

My Grief Cycle

Purpose

Acceptance

Anger
Depression

Faith
Love
Hope

Avoidance
Distraction
Denial

Shock
Disbelief
Sadness

However, grief didn't hit me the moment my mother died. Instead, my grief began when I realized my mother was dying, which was on her 78th birthday. Shock, disbelief, and sadness weighed on me from that moment on because I knew the inevitable would happen.

When my mother passed away, I acknowledged that she was no longer in pain and had gone to be with her Lord and Savior, Jesus Christ, but I did not give myself space to grieve. I distracted myself from the pain by going back to work in an attempt to return to some semblance of normalcy. And yet, when I pulled into the parking lot of my workplace, I couldn't stop crying. I knew that my management team and peers would greet me as I walked through the doors of my office, giving their condolences. Each time I heard, "I'm sorry for your loss," I would have to face once again the fact that my mom was no longer there.

The avoidance and distraction tactics I used all fit under the umbrella of denial. I was still in disbelief. I listened to the only voicemail recording I had left from my mother on repeat so I would never forget her voice. Then I beat myself up emotionally because I deleted her previous voicemails and the video chats she had left me. Those recordings I had taken for granted were now invaluable, and I could never get them back.

Anguish ensued, along with uncontrollable crying, and then my sadness turned to anger. I couldn't understand why my mother didn't live to be 100-plus years old. I already knew she had kept some secrets from me, but I often wondered how many. For example, why didn't she get a biopsy when she first discovered the tumor in her spine—when it was still as small as a blueberry? Why take a wait-and-see approach if she was in pain? Was she scared to have back surgery? Why didn't she talk to someone about her fears to analyze the risks and rewards of the surgery? If she'd had the tumor removed earlier, would she have lived longer?

I had to live with the fact I would never get the answers to my "whys" and "what ifs." It was too late for me to get the information I wanted to process my mother's death. I thought I would have more time with her. I thought her grandchildren had more time with her. We had just been laughing on my couch in North Carolina six months earlier, and now my mother was dead. I kept alternating back and forth between anger and shock.

Another issue I endured, along with my anger, was a constant struggle with depression. Before I began my journey toward healing, my go-to defense mechanism was to build an emotional wall any time I felt hurt. I had an all-or-nothing, throw-the-baby-out-with-the-bathwater mindset whenever I felt emotionally violated. I built a private fortress to protect me from pain, trauma, and rejection from others. However, that personal fortress led to isolation. I purposely separated myself from people who loved and cared about me, burying my emotions and never expressing how I felt. This self-imposed isolation caused me to become trapped in a vicious cycle of depression.

After my mother's death, I realized that part of my depression was due to unresolved trauma rooted in my childhood. The environment I grew up in didn't foster love or growth. I always felt that my life would have been better if my parents were never married. My parents were at their worst when they were together.

As a result of those childhood scars, I moved away from Houston as soon as I graduated from college. I thought I could run away from my childhood problems. However, I took my unhealed trauma bags with me wherever I went without realizing it and unintentionally recreated the same toxic environment I had grown up in as a child.

For years, I projected the pain of my dad's emotional abandonment onto my mother, which was not fair to her. I knew my mother loved me, but I felt that I had to work hard to be loved, respected, and validated by my dad. Love did not stand on its own with my dad. I felt I had to earn his love through my works and accomplishments. My dad was emotionally distant from my family as well and not intricately woven into its fabric like my mother. Even now, my children can recall childhood, teenage, and young adult memories they shared with their grandmother, but not their grandfather.

As I processed thoughts from my past, the question "What do I do now?" kept repeating in my head. I could no longer visit my mother at her home when I needed comfort. She wouldn't make any more quarterly visits to see me in North Carolina, bringing her suitcase full of ingredients, herbs, and vegetables to cook my favorite Trinidadian dishes. I would no longer smell her distinct fragrance or feel her embrace. That made me angry! But at the same time, I realized my anger would not serve me well for the remaining days I had left on this earth.

My mother's death awakened a longing within me to live a more purposeful life. My mother left a legacy of love, faith, and service, which made me question my own legacy. What values, ideas, and lessons would I leave my children? How could I live my life now in a way that would inspire my children to keep pushing forward, despite any obstacles they might face? My mother's handwritten journals drew me even closer to her after her death and inspired me to want more out of life. I was tired of surviving, and I wanted to live. But to live, I had to give myself permission to heal from my unhealed trauma.

Heal the Trauma

In April 2020, I started therapy with the goal of surrendering completely to the process. However, as the months went on, I found myself overwhelmed with a mixture of emotions all at once. I had to process my bereavement, deal with the impact of the COVID-19 pandemic, watch civil unrest on TV, and witness the fallout from a presidential election. That unprecedented moment in history forced the world to pause, and it also gave me the time I needed to unpack my childhood trauma. It was painful, but we can't heal what we don't address.

I wrote a series of questions in my journal that bubbled up in my spirit, questions I wanted to finally answer. I asked God to help me use this time of stillness during the pandemic to heal my brokenness and put the broken pieces back together within me.

Therapy notes

How to use my voice and speak clearly, defining boundaries and my wants when emotional. (how I am truly feeling)

*How to shift my brain from only remembering negative things and reliving the past and trauma over and over again.

* heal past wounds and trauma

* Practical way of grieving my mom's death

* how to deal with no communication with my Dad and inquiring about my siblings

Create in me a pure heart, O God,
and renew a steadfast spirit within me.
Psalm 51:10

*How to discover me all over again? - I have been taking care of everyone else but I need self care. Balance

I cut people off when I am mad; how do I communicate my hurt but still have compassion?

- How to use my voice and speak clearly, defining boundaries and my wants when emotional. (How am I truly feeling?)
- How to shift my brain from only remembering negative things and reliving the past and trauma over and over again?
- Heal past wounds and trauma
- Practical ways of grieving my mom's death
- How to deal with no communication from my dad and inquiring about my other siblings?

- How to discover me all over again? I have been taking care of every-one else, but I need self-care. (balance)
- I cut people off when I am mad. How do I communicate my hurt and still have compassion?

How ironic! The bottom of the journal page had a bible verse that spoke about the transformation and renewal of the spirit, which I had so desperately sought after since my mother's death.

> *Create in me a pure heart, O God, and renew a steadfast spirit within me.*

> (Psalms 51:10, NIV)

Healing my Inner Child was the first step in my journey to live my best life. The Inner Child is defined as a person's supposed original or true self, especially when regarded as damaged or concealed by negative childhood experiences.

We were all once children, and still have that child dwelling within us. But most adults are quite unaware of this. And this lack of conscious relatedness to our own inner child is precisely where so many behavioral, emotional and relationship difficulties stem from.

The fact is that the majority of so-called adults are not truly adults at all. We all get older. Anyone, with a little luck, can do that. But, psychologically speaking, this is not adulthood. True adulthood hinges on acknowledging, accepting, and taking responsibility for loving and parenting one's own inner child. For most adults, this never happens. Instead, their inner child has been denied, neglected, disparaged, abandoned, or rejected. We are told by society to "grow up," putting childish things aside. To become adults, we've been taught that our inner child— representing our child-like capacity for innocence, wonder, awe, joy, sensitivity, and playfulness—must be stifled, quarantined, or even killed. The inner child comprises and potentiates these positive qualities. But it also holds our accumulated childhood hurts, traumas, fears, and angers. "Grown-ups" are convinced they have successfully outgrown, jettisoned, and left this child—and its emotional baggage— long behind. But this is far from the truth. [2]

My Inner Child had been angry for quite some time. She would show up and show out in every way possible, complete with temper tantrums. I was notorious for throwing the baby out with the bathwater. If I felt hurt, everyone around me would hurt as well. My husband took the brunt of my misdirected anger. I brought my suitcases of unresolved trauma into my new marriage and dropped them into his lap as if he was responsible for taking away all my pain and anguish.

The communication in our marriage was horrible. Our words were like misfired missiles, our talking points never landing or resonating with each other. I snapped at my husband any time he questioned me. He felt like I didn't listen to him, and I felt like I had to fight with him to be respected and heard. I didn't trust him when he showed me grace and kindness; I always thought he was up to something. I never saw grace and compassion, only harsh criticism and the turmoil I had seen between my parents and experienced in my previous relationships. Conflict and defensiveness were normalized behavior patterns for me, and destructive thoughts wreaked havoc in my mind.

During one particular argument with my husband, I almost ended our marriage. I was sick and tired of being emotionally drained. Then, my husband asked me a simple question: "What is it you really want?" At first, I couldn't answer the question. Then, after I took a step back and re-flected on my heart's desire, I recognized the truth. I didn't want a divorce. I wanted to heal.

Fortunately, therapy dug up all the emotions I had buried and forced me to deal with them. I learned to heal my Inner Child by uncovering what had been hidden for so long. For the first time in my life, I cried for the little girl within me who had been misunderstood, emotionally neglected, and afraid. I allowed her to feel all the feels without putting up an emo-tional wall. I lay prostrate on the floor and let out a heart-filled cry, finally allowing my heart to break for my Inner Child. A heavy weight lifted off me when I did, and I released all the emotions I had buried over the years.

Later, I wrote a prayer in my journal, praising God for my tears be-cause I finally grieved for the little girl inside who had been dealing with unhealed trauma for far too long. I also prayed for God's guidance and for Him to be with me on my journey toward healing. The bible verses at the bottom of my journal pages seemed to speak directly to me.

Be strong and courageous. Do not be afraid; do not be discouraged, for the Lord your God will be with you wherever you go.

(Joshua 1:9)

"Be strong and courageous. The Lord your God will be
with you wherever you go."
Joshua 1:9

4/24/20

Thank you for the tears, Lord, as they wash the pain so I can feel and release. Teach me, Lord, how to let go of the trauma. I'm holding on too tight to it, and I cannot move. I'm clinging to it as a reminder of my past to protect myself when I really need to be hanging on to you for life, rest, and elevation. Lord, thank you for this journey you are taking me on, and I pray for healing in Jesus' name. Amen!

My therapy sessions seemed more like a college course in Life 101 because I had to unlearn learned behavior and let go of any attachments that no longer served me. In each session, I broke a chain of emotional bondage that was holding me back. My therapist and I tackled one topic per week. In between each session, I had homework to reflect on what we discussed and how it resonated with me. My homework affirmed that I had been playing myself small for far too long because of unhealed trauma.

Life Lesson 1: Address My Inner Critic. My Inner Critic reflected all the negative criticism I had heard and experienced as a child. I often dismissed positive life experiences and compliments and clung to the voice of my Inner Critic instead. My therapist reassured me that the Inner Critic was the problem, not me! She wanted me to disassociate myself from it by naming it. I decided to call my Inner Critic "Shady Boots."

If I wanted to deal with my Inner Critic, I had to acknowledge why she was in my head in the first place. "Shady Boots" could get crafty with her tongue and had a way of making me second guess myself. She was there to protect me from making mistakes, but I allowed her criticism to overshadow any good thing that happened in my life, and that criticism paralyzed me with fear. I had to face her head-on in order to walk fully in the purpose God had for my life.

These days, any time "Shady Boots" has something to say, I talk back to her, unequivocally proclaiming that "I am safe," "I am loved," and "I got this." I also remind myself, "I will ask for help and research the answers to my problems" instead of stewing in self-doubt and self-pity.

Life Lesson 2: Understand the Influence and Impact of the Generational Gap in My Family. My parents were from the Traditionalist Generation, better known as the Silent Generation. Children from the Silent Generation were expected to be seen and not heard. My parents had a one-size-fits-all toolbox of survival skills, which served them well as West Indian immigrants living in the United States. That toolbox focused on image and public perception and used what you did for a living as a litmus test for success.

I belonged to Generation X and was also a first-generation American. I was the opposite of a Traditionalist, and my survivor toolbox was foreign to my parents. I wanted to walk into uncharted territory discover more about myself and life. Unfortunately, my parent's skillset was incompatible with building my self-confidence, self-worth, or how I would define success for myself. I wanted my parents to show me new experiences and nurture my passions, but how could they teach me new experiences if they hadn't experienced new things themselves?

In therapy, I learned my mom and dad parented me out of their own unhealed trauma. I had to learn not to hold anger against them for what they did not know. As the poet Maya Angelou famously said, "When you know better, you do better."

The breakthrough I had about my parents led to my next lesson, which was forgiveness.

Life Lesson 3: Forgiveness. Domestic violence was a normalized experience for me as a young child, and as a result, my Inner Child was angry at my parents for the trauma I experienced. However, as an adult, I am responsible for my life; I am no longer a child living in my parents' home. I had to learn the process of forgiveness[3]. My therapist took me through forgiveness exercises and activities that taught me how to let go of the anger and resentment I carried toward everyone who mistreated me. I learned to treat them with compassion and recognized that it's okay to love people from a distance.

As I worked through the forgiveness exercises, I realized I was not just a victim; I was also an offender. I, too, have hurt people primarily because of unhealed trauma. I used to be highly critical and judgmental of other people, but in therapy, I realized that my parents' criticism made me critical of myself. In the same way, I became critical of others, judging them based on their flaws and imperfections, and I withheld grace and mercy from them. I was the definition of the saying, "Hurt people, hurt people," but it did not make my behavior justifiable.

Fortunately, once I learned to forgive myself, it became easier for me to forgive others. Holding onto anger did not serve me well, and it was killing my spirit.

> *When you're kind to others, you help yourself; when you're cruel to others, you hurt yourself.* (Proverbs 11:17, The Message)

Life Lesson 4: Stop the Negative Self-Talk. I had negative core beliefs[4] about myself, which I needed to dismantle. I had been attached to them for far too long, and my therapist helped me work through them. They had nothing to do with me but everything to do with my negative experiences and how people had negatively impacted me. My trauma-based mindset made me think that I was unworthy of anything good that happened to me. I had to learn to show myself compassion.

First, my therapist instructed me to research and write six self-affirmations that I could use to self-identify. Then, I set my alarm clock to go off six times per day. Each time the alarm rang, I read each affirmation out loud to speak positivity over my life. This process helped me turn the negative core beliefs I believed about myself into positive core beliefs. I also wrote these six self-affirmations in my journal, printed them out, and placed them on my vision board.

6 Affirmations

- I am more than the things I have told myself about myself! I am a Spirit expressing as a human being; I am unlimited!

- I release my attachment to everything that no longer serves me.

- I am worthy of Love. There is nothing that can change that. I was born worthy

- As I forgive myself, it becomes easier to forgive others.

- I deserve compassion,

The LORD your God is with you, He is mighty to save.
He will take great delight in you, He will quiet you with His love.
Zephaniah 3:17

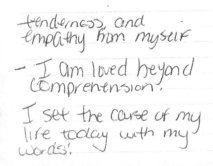

tenderness, and empathy from myself
– I am loved beyond comprehension.
I set the course of my life today with my words!

- I am more than the things I have told myself about myself! I am a spirit expressing as a human being; I am unlimited!
- I release my attachment to everything that no longer serves me.
- I am worthy of love. There is nothing that I can do to change that. I was born worthy.
- As I forgive myself, it becomes easier to forgive others.
- I deserve compassion, tenderness, and empathy from myself.
- I am loved beyond comprehension.

I set the course of my life today with my words!

In the beginning, it felt foreign for me to speak affirmations over myself. Until that moment, I had been dependent on other people to speak life over me. I had to ask myself, *why was I waiting on someone else to affirm me when I had the power to do it myself?* As difficult as it was at first, I eventually surrendered to the exercise and continued to speak positive words over my life. Each day I felt more empowered, and the words I spoke began to take root in my heart. The self-affirmation exercise taught me that my words have power and that I set the course of my life today with my words.

THRIVE IN LIFE

Life Lesson 5: Rediscovering Me.

For most of my life, I have worn pain as a badge of honor and tied my identity to it. I had a psychological badge for every traumatic event that had ever happened to me, and I didn't have enough room to hold all of them: Pain Badge, Single Mom Badge, Unemployed and Pregnant Badge, Childhood Trauma Badge, and Martyr Complex[5] Badge.

In order to heal, I could no longer shackle myself to the ball and chain of pain I had been dragging around all those years. I had to ask myself, "Who could I become on the other side of my healing process?" I needed to change my mindset and break free from my self-imposed shackles by bringing more joy back into my life.

As part of this process, my therapist gave me a homework assignment with one simple question: What brings me joy? I had to redefine what joy and happiness looked like for me, no one else but me! I wrote the answers in my journal:

What does happiness look
like for me?
- Leaving the past in the
past
- Healing from trauma
- Speaking with
authority
- Beliving I am...
        capable
    - intelligent
    - Qualified

Moments of Happiness
- Traveling to new places
- experiencing new cultures
- food
    - meeting new people

Reconnecting with nature
- beach & mountains
- walks, hikes, zoos

The Lord Himself goes before you and will be with you;
He will never leave you nor forsake you.
Deuteronomy 31:8

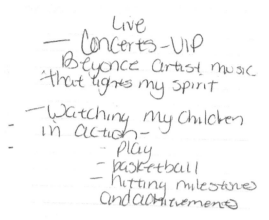

What does happiness look like for me?

- Leaving the past in the past
- Healing from trauma
- Speaking with authority
- Believing I am capable, intelligent, and qualified

Moments of Happiness:

- Traveling to new places, experience new cultures, food, and meeting new people
- Reconnecting with nature
- Beach & mountains
- Walks, hikes, zoos
- Live concerts—VIP (Beyonce, artists, music that lights my spirit)
- Watching my children in action—play, basketball, hitting milestones and achievements

Everything I described as things that brought me joy was attainable, but first, I had to allow myself to heal and let go of the attachments that no longer served me. Self-pity and happiness cannot occupy the same space. A negative plus a positive equals a negative.

In the middle of my cycle of grief, three things stuck with me: faith, love, and hope. My mother gave me all three of them. After her death, her journal writings wrapped around my heart, hugging me tightly as they provided faith, love, and hope. Physically, my mother may not be with me, but her energy never died. Her spirit has transcended to a supernatural state of being, and her words still guide and inspire me daily. My mother repeatedly said that she wished she had more to give me, but the truth was she gave me everything. She gave me love.

> *And now these three remain: faith, hope, and love. But the greatest of these is love.*
>
> (1 Corinthians 13:13, NIV)

Chapter 11

Your Journey to Healing

I created *The Day My Heart Turned Blue Bereavement Companion Journal* to be used in conjunction with this book, *The Day My Heart Turned Blue: Healing After the Loss of My Mother*. The companion journal is designed to help the bereaved make space to heal, reflect, and honor the loss of a loved one so they can move forward. As you go through the journal, I encourage you to write your thoughts and life experiences. Don't be afraid to be unapologetically raw and honest in your writing, no matter how difficult the pain might be right now. When you pour out your heart on paper, you shine a light on the darkest emotions you may experience in your state of sorrow, which helps you work through them.

You are the author of your life. Consider using this journal as a memoir documenting your healing journey after your parent's death. In your pain, you may feel like there are days you are climbing a relentless mountain with an enormous weight on your back. Be encouraged. Your life may feel like a mess, but this so-called mess will give way to an inspirational message that you can share to encourage others. That's what happened to me.

On October 28th, 2020, I decided to start my own business as an author, personal development coach, and speaker. I no longer wanted to allow fear to rob me of my present or my future. I asked God to guide me along the way and help me celebrate my accomplishments. Until that point in my life, I struggled to celebrate myself, whether it involved birthdays or other milestones. I never thought I deserved anything other than pain. I had to decide to heal the innermost parts of myself so that I could thrive.

Delight yourself in the Lord and He will give you the desires of your heart. Psalm 37:4

10/28/20 - 1:10pm

Heavenly father, I thank you for this day — I have been having digestive issues, heartburn, and sleepless nights I know it is contributed to the emotions and excitement of starting a new business. Lord, guide my hand and thoughts — I need to give myself permission to celebrate accomplishments and most importantly revel in the awe of you! — Thank you Lord for all that you have done. Thank you for the community of family + friends especially during a pandemic — Your hand can be seen through it all. Lord, I lift myself, my business,

Pleasant words are like a honeycomb, sweet to the soul and healing to the bones... Proverbs 16:24

this nation, this word to
you! My I accept the
orders you give me to be
a light in a dark place—
Please tell mommy hello
for me and that I love &
miss her! God you are
good and your mercy
endureth forever! Please
help me to give the same
advice to myself that
I give to others—
rest, lean into the uncertainty
with faith; God is in control!
In Jesus name, Amen!

10/28/20 - 1:10PM

Heavenly Father, I thank you for this day. I have been having digestive issues, heartburn, and sleepless nights. I know it is contributed to the emotions and excitement of starting a new business. Lord, guide my hand and thoughts. I need to give myself permission to celebrate accomplishments and, most importantly, revel in the awe of you! Thank you, Lord, for all that you have done! Thank you for the community of family and friends, especially during a pandemic. Your hand can be seen through it all! Lord, I lift myself, my business, this nation, this world to you! May I accept the orders you give me to be a light in a dark place. Please tell Mommy hello for me and that I love and miss her! God, you are good, and your mercy endures forever! Please help me to give the same advice to myself that I give to others; rest, lean into the uncertainty with faith; God is in control! In Jesus' name, Amen!

Once I moved from surviving to thriving in life, my creativity began to overflow. I looked at problems not through a trauma-based lens but as opportunities to stretch and use my unique abilities. On November 16th, 2020, I completed the Coach Training Intensive taught by the Coaching and Positive Psychology Institute. During this training, I had an idea to create journals for my business that included guided questions and space for clients to write notes and homework during the coaching sessions. I wrote this idea in my journal, and its manifestation came to fruition six months later.

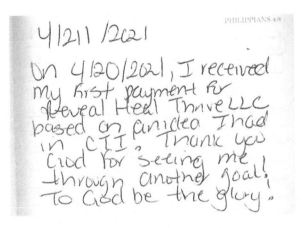

04/21/2021

On 4/20/2021, I received my first payment for Reveal Heal Thrive LLC based on an idea I had in CTI! Thank you, God, for seeing me through another goal! To God be the glory!

I've benefited a great deal from writing out my pain and victories in my journals. It is truly amazing to see something you wrote weeks, months, or even years ago transform from words into action. It wasn't until I found my mother's journals that detailed her prayers, deeds, and actions that I became inspired to write this book and a companion journal. I hope reading *The Day My Heart Turned Blue* inspires you to purchase *The Day My Heart Turned Blue Bereavement Companion Journal* as well. And I hope the journal shines a light on the areas where you need to heal so that you can move from surviving to thriving in life.

Acknowledgements

Heavenly Father, thank you for guiding me. Thank you for your Holy Spirit working through me to write encouraging words for your children who are grappling with the loss of their loved ones. Thank you for being a beacon of hope on days that seem bleak because of despair. You are the Great Comforter. Thank you for strengthening me when I doubted myself or thought I didn't have the skills to bring this project to life.

> *But he said to me, "My grace is sufficient for you, for my power is made perfect in weakness." Therefore, I will boast all the more gladly about my weaknesses so that Christ's power may rest on me. That is why, for Christ's sake, I delight in weaknesses, in insults, in hardships, in persecutions, in difficulties. For when I am weak, then I am strong.*
>
> (2 Corinthians 12:9-11, NIV)

Thank you, Heavenly Father, for planting the seeds of creativity, gratitude, and excellence within me that birthed *The Day my Heart Turned Blue* and the companion journal. This writing process has been a beautiful journey rooted in love, honor, and reverence for my mother, Eutrice E. James.

I am thankful for my mother, who brought me into this world despite the many obstacles she faced. Mommy, your love surrounds me daily. I am so grateful for everything you've done for me while here on earth. I miss your physical presence, but I know you are with me in spirit and that we will meet again. I love you!

To my husband, Demarcus: Thank you for your continued support, love, and devotion, and for being with me while my mother took her last breath. I know it was difficult to come alongside me as I mourned since it reminded you of the untimely passing of your mother, whom I never had the pleasure of meeting. I genuinely believe these unfortunate events brought us closer together and solidified our bond as husband and wife. May God bless you seven times over for the kindness and comfort you showed me in my grief. I love you so much!

> *My beloved is mine, and I am his...*
>> (Song of Solomon 2:16, NIV)

To my children, Dischon, Dorell, Dinari, and Dylan: I thank God for allowing me to be your mother. I broke the generational curse of unhealed trauma within our family so that you don't have to. I am so proud of the young men you have become. I pray you are just as proud of yourself as I am of you. Each one of you will be an unstoppable force in all your pursuits when you align your desires with God's will. Continue to speak God's promises over your life and watch God move in ways you could never imagine.

> *Take delight in the Lord, and he will give you the desires of your heart.*
>> (Psalms 37:4, NIV)

To Dinari, my bonus son, my love for you is not by birth but from the heart. May God cover you in your journey to adulthood as you forge your path and redefine who you are in Christ!

> *For we are God's handiwork, created in Christ Jesus to do good works, which God prepared in advance for us to do.*
>> (2 Corinthians 5:17, NIV)

To my precious Trini family: I am forever connected to you through my mother and her beloved country of Trinidad and Tobago. Auntie Jennifer and Uncle Martin, there are not enough words to express how grateful I am for all that you did for my mother during those painful last months of her life. To all my Trini aunts, uncles, cousins, and those friends we call family: I thank you for your prayers and encouragement.

To the "Golden Girls," Ms. Louise and Ms. Gloria: There hasn't been a better-looking duo of grown, fun-loving, and opinionated women whom I adore. Thank you for being Mommy's best friends.

To my mother's beloved Sagemont Church: Sagemont will always be dear to my heart because I accepted Christ as my Savior at ten years old during a Sagemont children's church service. Thank you for all the love you showed my mother over the years. She truly enjoyed her time at retreats, on mission trips, and sewing dresses for all those in need. Those experiences were all made possible because of Sagemont Church. I am also grateful for all the friendships my mother gained through Sagemont. I felt your love for her from the stories she shared with me about you and through her journal writings.

Thank you to all my friends, colleagues, and the mothers who sent texts, cards, gifts, lifted my family in prayer, and attended my mother's funeral or visited her at her bedside.

Thank you to all my mother's friends, neighbors, and all who had the pleasure of meeting her. My heart is full of gratitude for your kind-heartedness during our family's time of grief.

God bless you all.

Thank you for reading *The Day My Heart Turned Blue: Healing After the Loss of My Mother*. I encourage you to leave an honest review at your favorite online bookstore so that others who have suffered a loss will be encouraged to read it as well. Gaining exposure as an independent author relies mostly on word-of-mouth, so if you have the time and desire, please consider leaving a short review wherever you can.

You can also subscribe to my mailing list at www.revealhealthrive.com to find out about upcoming books, events, and more!

Love,
Karla J. Noland

Endnotes

CHAPTER 1

1. Rajesh Balakrishnan, Rokeya Porag, Dewan Shamsul Asif, A. M. Rejaus Satter, Md. Taufiq, Samson S. K. Gaddam, "Primary Intracranial Melanoma with Early Leptomeningeal Spread: A Case Report and Treatment Options Available," *Case Reports in Oncological Medicine*, vol. 2015, Article ID 293802, 7 pages, 2015. https://www.hindawi.com/journals/crionm/2015/293802/

CHAPTER 2

1. "What services are not covered under Medicare Part B?" *AARP*, Last modified March 29, 2017, https://www.aarp.org/health/medicare-qa-tool/services-not-covered-by-medicare-part-b/
2. Jennifer J. Salopek, "Medicaid Coverage for Nursing Homes: Don't 'Spend Down' Without a Plan," *AARP*, October 24, 2019, https://www.aarp.org/caregiving/financial-legal/info-2019/medicaid-nursing-home-coverage.html
3. "What is Hospice Care?" *American Cancer Society*, Last modified on May 10, 2019, https://www.cancer.org/treatment/end-of-life-care/hospice-care/what-is-hospice-care.html

CHAPTER 4

1. Jessica Koth, "2019 NFDA General Price List Study Shows Funeral Costs Not Rising As Fast As Rate of Inflation," *National Funeral Directors*

Association, December 19, 2019, https://nfda.org/news/media-center/nfda-news-releases/id/4797/2019-nfda-general-price-list-study-shows-funeral-costs-not-rising-as-fast-as-rate-of-inflation

2. "Texas Probate Guide," *Forbes & Forbes Law*, December 21, 2018, https://www.forbeslawoffice.com/probate/texas-probate-guide/

3. "The Probate Process," *American Bar Association*, Last modified on August 8, 2021, https://www.americanbar.org/groups/real_property_trust_estate/resources/estate_planning/the_probate_process/

CHAPTER 6

1. Carol A. Lambert, MSW, "6 Troubling Signs of Psychological Abuse in a Relationship: Psychological abuse endangers women with 'hidden injuries,'" *Psychology Today*, August 30, 2017, https://www.psychologytoday.com/us/blog/mind-games/201708/6-troubling-signs-psychological-abuse

CHAPTER 7

1. "Ctrl-Alt-Del," *PC Mag*, Last modified on August 8, 2021, https://www.pcmag.com/encyclopedia/term/ctrl-alt-del

CHAPTER 8

1. Joel Osteen, *Daily Readings from Next Level Thinking: 90 Devotions for a Successful and Abundant Life*, (New York: FaithWords, 2019).

CHAPTER 10

1. Christina Gregory, Ph.D., "The Five Stages of Grief: An Examination of the Kubler-Ross Model," *Psycom*, Last modified May 4, 2021, https://www.psycom.net/depression.central.grief.html

2. Stephen A. Diamond Ph.D., "Essential Secrets of Psychotherapy: The Inner Child," *Psychology Today*, June 7, 2008, https://www.psychologytoday.com/us/blog/evil-deeds/200806/essential-secrets-psychotherapy-the-inner-child

3. "Forgiveness Therapy," *Therapist Aid*, Last modified on August 9, 2021, https://www.therapistaid.com/therapy-worksheet/forgiveness-therapy

4. Seth J. Gillihan Ph.D., "What Makes Us Think Such Negative Things About Ourselves?" *Psychology Today*, February 14, 2018, https://www.psychologytoday.com/us/blog/think-act-be/201802/what-makes-us-think-such-negative-things-about-ourselves

5. Sharon Martin, LCSW, "The Martyr Complex: How to Stop Feeling Like a Victim and Create Healthy Relationships," *Psych Central*, October 15, 2016, https://www.psychcentral.com/blog/imperfect/2016/10/martyr-complex-how-to-stop-feeling-like-a-victim-create-healthy-relationships#The-opposite-of-martyrdom-is-expressing-your-needs

Resources

MENTAL HEALTH ORGANIZATIONS

- **NAMI** - NAMI is the National Alliance on Mental Illness, the nation's largest grassroots mental health organization dedicated to building better lives for the millions of Americans affected by mental illness. https://www.nami.org
- **HelpGuide** - HelpGuide is a small independent nonprofit that runs one of the world's top 10 mental health websites. Over 50 million people worldwide turn to HelpGuide each year for trustworthy content they can use to improve their mental health and make healthy changes. https://www.helpguide.org/

FIND A THERAPIST

- **Therapy for Black Girls** - Therapy for Black Girls is an online space dedicated to encouraging the mental wellness of Black women and girls. https://therapyforblackgirls.com
- **Psychology Today** - Psychology Today is the world's largest mental health and behavioral science destination online. It is the world's largest portal to psychotherapy; it includes free access to thousands of professionals. https://www.psychologytoday.com

FAMILY CAREGIVING

- **AARP** - AARP is the nation's largest nonprofit, nonpartisan organization dedicated to empowering Americans 50 and older to choose how they live as they age. https://www.aarp.org/
- **National Hospice and Palliative Care Organization** - CaringInfo, a National Hospice and Palliative Care Organization program, provides free resources to help people make decisions about end-of-life care and services before a crisis. https://www.nhpco.org/

The Day My Heart Turned Blue
Bereavement Companion Journal

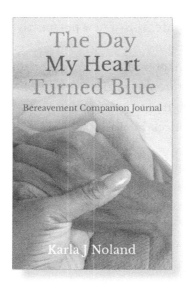

The Day My Heart Turned Blue Bereavement Companion Journal is meant to complement Karla J. Noland's book, *The Day My Heart Turned Blue: Healing After the Loss of My Mother*. However, it can also be used on its own to guide you on your bereavement journey. The purpose of the companion journal is to guide the bereaved through the process of healing, reflecting, and honoring their parent so they can move forward.

The journal is composed of three parts:

Part 1: Embracing Your Emotions. This section will walk you through a cathartic experience of identifying and releasing the range of powerful emotions triggered by the loss of a parent. Grief cannot be stifled or rushed. You need to allow yourself to experience all of the emotions in order to get to the other side. And you get to decide what the other side of grief looks like for you.

Part 2: Self-Care for a Grieving Heart. This section outlines the four steps of bereavement self-care that can help you heal from a wounded heart. Grief can have an unshakeable hold on your heart when you lose a loved one. Mourning ensues because your heart is devastated, and you realize that what was no longer is. Fortunately, with proper care, a wounded heart can heal.

Part 3: Honoring your Loved One. This section will coach you through the process of moving forward by celebrating your loved one's heavenly birthday, getting through the holiday season, and turning your pain into purpose. You can view life from a new perspective as you heal, one that is full of hope and inspiration.

In between each chapter of the companion journal, you will find self-check-ins that prompt you to perform emotional checkups on yourself. The check-ins are designed to provide you with valuable personal insight into your current emotional state and allow you to reflect on the progress you've made.

Remember that you are the author of your life. Your journal should be unapologetically raw and honest, no matter how difficult the pain is right now. When you pour your heart out on paper, you shine a light on the darkest emotions you may experience due to your grief. You might even consider turning this journal into a memoir documenting your healing journey after your parent's death. Some days, it may feel like you're climbing a relentless mountain with an enormous amount of weight on your back. Be encouraged. Your life may feel like a mess, but this so-called mess will give way to an inspirational message for you to share to encourage others.

May the therapeutic power of journaling in *The Day My Heart Turned Blue Bereavement Companion Journal* allow you to reveal the areas in your life where you need to heal the most, so you can move from surviving grief to thriving in life.

You can purchase *The Day My Heart Turned Blue Bereavement Companion Journal* at www.revealhealthrive.com or anywhere books and eBooks are sold.

About The Author

Karla J. Noland is a wife, working mom, author, certified personal development coach, and speaker who loves sharing what she has learned. Her mission is to help working mothers prioritize themselves and their dreams at the top of their to-do lists, and create a winning strategy to achieve their goals.

Karla established Reveal Heal Thrive LLC in October 2020 after the untimely passing of her mother. She spent much of her life holding on to pain, trauma, and anger, and as part of her healing process, Karla recognized that she was merely surviving in life but was not thriving. She wanted to live a more purposeful life and let go of any attachments that no longer served her. Over time, Karla turned her adversity into opportunity, and thus Reveal Heal Thrive LLC was born.

Today, Karla lives in Durham, North Carolina, with her husband and sons.

- Instagram: @revealhealthrive
- Facebook: @revealhealthrive
- Twitter: @rhthrive
- YouTube: @revealhealthrive
- Sign up for the Reveal Heal Thrive blog at www.revealhealthrive. com/blog to read more inspirational and informative content centered on personal development, mental health, and living your best life.

Reveal Heal Thrive Personal Development Coaching

MISSION

Reveal Heal Thrive Personal Development Coaching helps working mothers prioritize themselves and their dreams at the top of their to-do lists with winning strategies to achieve their goals.

VISION

Reveal Heal Thrive Personal Development Coaching seeks to inspire working mothers to give themselves permission to pursue their goals and dreams. Our goal is to build confidence, provide clarity, and increase capability with each breakthrough that happens by helping women combine their unique superpowers and values to achieve their goals.

PURPOSE

I believe overcoming trials and tribulations has made you resilient and made it possible for you to manifest your purpose through your pain. Maybe you've lived in survival mode and believed the lies you've told yourself. You've held onto the false narrative that it's too late, you don't have what it takes, or you're selfish to pursue your dreams. I've been there. I put everyone else ahead of myself and forgot who I was until I got help. If this is your struggle, I can help. Let me teach you how to give yourself permission to hope, dream, and achieve your goals. Learn more at https://revealhealthrive.com/coaching

Made in the USA
Middletown, DE
03 November 2023

41807271R00073